Advance praise for
Thriving as a Broker in the 21st Century
by Thomas J. Dorsey

"Tom Dorsey has written a very insightful treatise about the broker of the 21st century. His comments serve as **a roadmap to success for brokers of all ages and experience**. I am very glad our paths crossed!"

> JOHN SHERMAN
> President & CEO
> Scott & Stringfellow

"Tom Dorsey's latest literary endeavor will help take brokers 'out of the box'. Much more than a testament to Point and Figure analysis, **this book presents thoughts and ideas of successful professionals brought to the forefront by the unique Dorsey style**. *Thriving as a Broker in the 21st Century* is 'value-added' and a must-read for the investment community."

> JOHN FELBER
> Partner
> J. C. Bradford & Co.

"This book . . . begins where it should—with relationships. **It emphasizes the absolute basics of loving the business, establishing a solid game plan, and being willing to work hard**. All of which is rooted in understanding risk. This wonderful book ends with the best advice of all—timing your purchases and sales and buying on pullbacks."

> RALPH J. ACAMPORA, CMT
> Managing Director & Director of Technical Research
> Prudential Securities Incorporated

Thriving as a Broker in the 21st Century

BLOOMBERG PROFESSIONAL LIBRARY

THOMAS J. DORSEY

Thriving as a Broker in the 21st Century

BLOOMBERG PRESS

PRINCETON

Books are available for bulk purchases at special discounts. Special editions or book excerpts can also be created to specifications. For information, please write: Special Markets Department, Bloomberg Press.

This publication contains the author's opinions and is designed to provide accurate and authoritative information. It is sold with the understanding that the author, publisher, and Bloomberg L.P. are not engaged in rendering legal, accounting, investment-planning, or other professional advice. The reader should seek the services of a qualified professional for such advice; the author, publisher, and Bloomberg L.P. cannot be held responsible for any loss incurred as a result of specific investments or planning decisions made by the reader.

First edition published 1999
1 3 5 7 9 10 8 6 4 2

Dorsey, Thomas J.
    Thriving as a broker in the 21st century / by Thomas J. Dorsey.
      p.   cm.
    Includes index.
    ISBN 1-57660-066-1 (alk. paper)
    1. Stockbrokers. I. Title.
HG4621.D67   1999
332.63'22–dc21   99-28640
                                                     CIP

Acquired and edited by Jacqueline R. Murphy

Book design by Don Morris Design

To my wife, Cindy, and children Thomas, Mitchell, & Samantha

CONTENTS

Introduction 1

Acknowledgments

WHAT A WONDERFUL EXPERIENCE it was working with the Bloomberg Publishing group. Without a doubt, this was the best experience I have had working with a publisher; the dedicated team at Bloomberg is nothing but the best. In particular it was Chris Graja, an editor of *Bloomberg Personal Finance* magazine and coauthor of *Investing in Small-Cap Stocks,* also published by Bloomberg Press, who first saw the potential for this book. Chris recommended to the publishers that they pursue the project. Once we started production, Jacquelyn Murphy and Melissa Hafner were instrumental in keeping the flow of this work organized. They kept encouraging me through the whole process—especially on the days when I thought the end would never be in sight. Jared Kieling was a tremendous help in guiding me and shaping the book with his in-depth understanding of the publishing process and book layout. His guidance was immeasurable. Other members of the great team I came in contact with were Karen Cook, Barbara Diez, Lisa Goetz, Christina Palumbo, Priscilla Treadwell, and Maris Williams.

Without Dennis Johnson I would never have made it through this process. Dennis is a court reporter and owner of Johnson & Associates in Richmond, Virginia. I started on this book with the thought that I would transcribe the interviews myself, as each one was conducted—I even bought a court reporter's transcription machine. Boy, was I dead wrong. It didn't take long to realize that there is much more to transcribing audiotapes than being a fast typist. Dennis offered his services to me free of charge. He worked in his spare time transcribing the interviews as I brought them back from my travels—a monumental job that Dennis performed unwaveringly. I owe Dennis a major debt of gratitude for being such a great friend when I was in need.

Tammy Derosier, my right-hand person at Dorsey, Wright, was also instrumental in keeping me on an even keel. Her organizational skills and tireless dedication to detail were key in completing this book. She was also a major help with my first book. Tammy is Vice President of Dorsey, Wright and one of the top analysts on Wall Street. Helping me with this book came on top of her normal corporate duties.

Last, but certainly not least, I would like to thank my wonderful family: my wife, Cindy, and three children, Thomas, Mitchell, and Samantha. They went weekends and nights without a husband and father as I slowly but surely inched my way to the finish line. None of this would have happened if Cindy hadn't prodded me and supported me along the way over the past twenty years. I would never have believed I could write one book, much less two, but she saw something in me I could not see in myself. I'm already planning the third.

INTRODUCTION

THRIVING AS A BROKER IN THE 21ST CENTURY

THE MOMENT I WAS introduced to Point and Figure charting, I understood the shape the rest of my career would take. That direction, I knew, was to teach my fellow brokers to become better at managing equities in order to make their clients more money. For the past twelve years I have run my own company with my partner, Watson Wright. In this time we have taught hundreds of seminars on Point and Figure analysis.

At Dorsey, Wright & Associates we advise over 250 broker dealers daily on Point and Figure technical analysis and in most cases function as the technical analysis department of these firms. During the past twelve years we have gotten to know many stockbrokers at scores of different firms. Our phones are open to any of our clients each day for consultation on anything from technical analysis to option strategies.

Because we have such close contact with the investment community, we have come to know the brokers whom we consider to be the best in the business. My only regret is that this book can't be thousands of pages long to include all of the stockbrokers I consider a cut above. This book is designed to arm the professional stockbroker with new ideas. The interviews I present herein are intended to offer a fresh approach for brokers who wish to increase the amount and quality of business they currently achieve.

One of the shared traits you'll see in all the stockbrokers interviewed here is their tremendous work ethic. They are all focused on success. Without this above-average drive, nothing other than a tremendous amount of family money can make a broker successful. You'll see differences, however, in the type of business each has built. Each one applies his or her trade a little differently from the others. This is why the book should be helpful to almost any stockbroker who reads it.

Although my company is a technical analysis firm, this book is not designed to teach technical analysis or to promote its relevance. The book is structured to help stockbrokers become better and more successful at managing and developing their business. It was written to ease their transition into the 21st century, during which their biggest competitor just might be their customers.

The brokers presented in this book were not chosen for the amount of production they generate. They were selected because they are craftsmen. Although the majority of those interviewed are high producers, that fact was not a determining criteria. I was interested in two things:

◆ the quality of their business

◆ their knowledge of the business.

Each broker interviewed has a unique, logical, and organized way of going about business; the end result in every case is customer satisfaction.

I entered the scene as a stockbroker in the 1970s.

Chapter 1 tells my story to set the stage for the rest of the book. As my high school teachers will tell you, I was not originally destined for finance, so I hope my own story will provide some bit of inspiration.

Chapter 2, "The Art of Prospecting," addresses one of the most vital parts of our business. Without a strong approach for generating new customers, a broker cannot flourish. Prospecting is partially a numbers game and partially an experiment in sociology. You need to have the ambition to contact a large number of leads, but you also have to make a personal connection in order to close the deal. I interviewed two brokers who prospect in very different ways—I would say one uses a rifle approach and the other a shotgun. Both are successful business generators.

Larry Pettit of Scott & Stringfellow shares some formulas to determine if you are on track with production goals and to calculate how many new assets you need to stay ahead. Neile Wolfe of Prudential Securities has developed an incredible business by capturing corporate stock option programs. He discusses how he goes about securing the big accounts.

Chapter 3, "Building Relationships," addresses one of the keys to maintaining longevity in this business. Because investors can get so much free investment information on the Internet, an imperative for maintaining business is strengthening relationships with clients. The broker I selected for this chapter is Jim DeMent, who works at Davenport & Company in Richmond. I have known Jim for twenty-four years, and I've watched as he carefully and skillfully manages relationships. His prospecting days are over because of the relationships he built early in his career.

Chapter 4, "Bringing Value to the Table," is about offering your clients much more than a laundry list of your firm's recommended stocks. Dennis Nelson of U.S. Bancorp Piper Jaffray describes his visionary method of combining value investing with technical analysis. This strategy is called "ValTech," and the returns he has given his clients over the years have been exemplary. In the same chapter, Chris Guttilla of Lehman Brothers discusses how he monitors insider transactions and uses technical and fundamental analysis to select the right stocks.

Because of today's increasingly competitive finance markets, many successful brokers have developed alternative methods to help clients reach their financial goals. They've managed to set themselves apart by specializing on a specific segment or by excelling at a particular strategy. Chapter 5, "Establishing Your Niche," describes how some brokers are able to capitalize on being different.

Sam Lee of Salomon Smith Barney is an asset allocator who uses risk management techniques to determine which money managers his clients should be working with at any given time in the market. He does not manage the money himself but he actively manages when his clients' funds should be in the markets. Scott Bowers of Paine Webber has carved out a niche working with small CPAs to help them provide investment services to their clients. In doing so, Scott has also increased his own business.

The reality of today's business environment is that belonging to one of the top three brokerage firms isn't the tremendous advantage it once was. With the advent of the Internet, it is increasingly easy for brokers to start their own operations and clear their trades through the firms where they previously worked. Chapter 6, "Starting Your Own Firm," offers advice from two thriving brokers who moved out on their own. Tim Daly of The Weston Group suggests that it's a cinch to hang out one's shingle, and he tells us why it's the best move he's ever made. Robert Cluck of The Aspen Equity Group has a less sanguine message. I wanted to provide both sides to this story.

Partnerships will become a strategic reality for many brokers as we enter the 21st century. It is becoming increasingly difficult to be all things to all people. Partnerships provide the way to become a one-stop shop without sacrificing customer service. In Chapter 7, "Building Partnerships," I interviewed brokers from two of the most successful partnerships I've come in contact with: Edward Rosenberg, David Rosenberg, and Richard Angelotti of Morgan Keegan & Co., and Nikki Chicotel and Sheila Burke of First Security Van Kasper. The partners in these firms expertly manage their segments of the business and have built a real trust with their counterparts. As a result, their clients have the benefit of diverse expertise.

Chapter 8, "Using Technical Analysis," covers one of my favorite topics. Again, this book is not intended to be a guide for using technical methods. But it is necessary to have a chapter on this subject nonetheless, because it is one of the most important parts of successful equity management. All brokers should consider adding it to their repertoire. I talked with two brokers who combine the Point and Figure method with strong fundamental analysis as the backbone of their strategy. Craig Wiener of PaineWebber and Jim Parrish of Morgan Keegan tell you how they do it.

Chapter 9, "The Making of a Financial Ministry" was the toughest chapter to prepare. I know quite a few successful and talented brokers, but Bob Woodall of Dain Rauscher stands out in so many ways—I would give my family account to Bob without a second thought. He is a broker with varied talents that stretch beyond finance but are applicable to his business.

Many investors are becoming acutely aware that 80 percent of money managers never outperform the S&P 500. Passive investing is becoming more prevalent, and investors are becoming more educated in the investment process. All these things make it more difficult for a broker to find and keep clients. I hope this book provides some new insights that help you build a bigger and more solid business. The stockbrokers within these pages open their businesses up to you in an unselfish attempt to help you become more successful. If you get one new idea that helps achieve better results in your business, then the cost of this book was a wise investment.

MY OWN
PERSPECTIVE

A STOCKBROKER IS PROBABLY the last thing my high

school teachers would have guessed I would become. I

think they suspected I would enter an occupation that

did not require an education. You see, I barely made it

through high school. As the son of an army officer, the

only occupation I ever considered was to become an

army officer myself. Being an "army brat" was a detri-

ment to my education but a benefit to my social life.

I was in nineteen different schools in my life, some for as short as six months. Every Christmas and birthday brought new remote-controlled tanks, rifles, army clothes, and the like. The only game we ever played was "army," and the only children I played with were other army dependents. I had very little contact with civilian children. In 1966 I graduated high school in Germany and began undergraduate school at Richard Bland College in Petersburg, Virginia.

It didn't take me long to flunk out. In fact, I lasted just one semester. My timing was impeccable, as this was the middle of the Vietnam War—you either earned a "C" average in college or you went into the service. I joined the navy in 1967 with the intention of going into underwater demolition. By my second day in boot camp I understood the value of a college education. I had to pay for my academic failure with four years of my life. In retrospect, I can see that those years presented some of the most significant experiences of my life. I desperately needed the education in life's skills that the navy provided.

When I was honorably discharged in 1970, Richard Band College gave me a second chance. After four years of sampling what life was like without an education, I was ready to get back to work and to do whatever it took to get that degree. I was on the same path my father followed. It wasn't until after WWII that he finally got his G.E.D. He received a battlefield commission before he finished twelfth grade.

He got his college degree the hard way, going to night school for ten years. In fact, I attended his college graduation when I was 13 years old.

When my education began the second time, the war in Vietnam was winding down and there were plenty of veterans returning to school. But getting used to academia wasn't easy. I hadn't read a book in four years and my reading skills had suffered. It took me four times longer than other students to complete an assignment—but I was determined. I arranged my classes in the morning so I would have all day to study.

I always remembered one of my father's favorite sayings: "Life's a cinch by the inch; life's hard by the yard." And inch by inch I made it to the Dean's List. I realized then that the key to success was confidence, and that was exactly what I was building in myself as I inched through college.

After a year or so I transferred about twenty-five miles up the road to Virginia Commonwealth University. The tuition was right—and since I was on the GI Bill, that was a chief concern. My major was business administration, but I loved economics so much that I took all my electives in that subject and ended up with two degrees. It wasn't until my senior year that I decided to become a stockbroker. I had no idea what a stockbroker did, I just knew he was close to the money, and that's where I wanted to be.

I sent my résumé to Merrill Lynch, but they weren't impressed with my four years' experience as an enlisted man in the navy. I had no idea that the stock market had just gone through a painful bear market. No one mentioned that in school. I had no concept of a bull or bear market, or even of recession. I wasn't qualified or ready to enter finance.

I finally accepted a job at Richard's Wine Cellars in Petersburg, Virginia, as a production supervisor. It was a great job: seventy hours a week earned me $8,000 a year and one free bottle of unpalatable wine per week. Richard's, a subsidiary of Canandaigua, was a very large and profitable company. It wasn't until years later when I watched Canandaigua's stock skyrocket that I realized the full potential of that job. The founder of Canandaigua, Max Sands, took to me as though I were his son. He was a very old man who never missed a day of work in his life.

Eventually I was transferred to the winery division where I met a wonderful man named Otto Selig, the winemaker. He was one of the top executives at the winery and the final word when it came to a finished product. He was a gentle man who thought every college kid was a half-wit, so none of the young guys working with Otto ever lasted very long. I think I might have been the first. He took to me just as Max had. In fact, I used to call Otto my second father. He taught me all about making wine, and I even began to envision a lasting career in the business.

It was sometime around the summer of 1974 that a good friend of mine, Dan Thompson, told me that Merrill, Lynch, Pierce,

Fenner & Smith was hiring again. Dan had just returned from a career weekend for Vietnam veterans and had interviewed with Merrill. Although he wasn't interested in becoming a broker, he suggested that I start banging on their door again to see if this time I might get in.

I sent my résumé up to the Richmond office and began a systematic telephone campaign of harassment aimed at the branch manager, Jim Crocker. I phoned every week to see if he had seen my résumé and made a decision. I felt sure that I would be hired. I was so unshakably certain that I resigned from Richard's Wine Cellars in anticipation of getting a start date from Crocker. Mac Sands (the winery founder) was extremely upset with my resignation, but I wasn't looking back. I had a 21-foot-sailboat at the time and decided to take a week's vacation and sail down the James River to Norfolk while I awaited an offer.

"I had no idea what a stockbroker did, I just knew he was close to the money, and that's where I wanted to be."

THOMAS DORSEY

Tuesday rolled around and it was time for my weekly call to Jim Crocker. He asked me to come in the following Tuesday to talk. Perseverance had paid off. I knew that if I could get in front of him I was in. When I went to the interview Mr. Crocker asked what my shortcomings were. Believe it or not I couldn't think of any. Lord knows, I have plenty of faults, but when posed with the question I went completely blank.

He didn't have any more questions for me so I assumed I had wasted my only chance. I'll never forget what he said next: "I'm going to offer you $900 a month, and we'll bargain down from there. What do you want to do?" I accepted immediately.

My only job in the beginning was to study and pass the Series 7 exam. Having recently graduated from college, the study part came easily and I loved every minute of it. On the Wednesday after the exam, I learned I had passed. That was one of the proudest moments of my life. I was now registered to represent for what I considered to be the greatest institution in the world, The New York Stock Exchange.

Once we got back to the office, the fanfare was over, and it was back to ground zero. Although we were registered, we newly hired employees didn't know much about the investment process. We weren't told that most investors had just been wiped out in the bear market of 1973–74. Meanwhile, we were prospecting leads who didn't even want to hear the word *stockbroker*. I can't tell you how many hundreds of phones were slammed on me.

My marketing plan was simple. I purchased a directory that listed every Virginia executive, and I began dialing the names that started with Z. I knew the other new brokers had the same book and were starting with A. That was my grand strategy! Jim Crocker wanted production—and I realized that in addition to prospecting, I had to become an expert in some facet of the business. Options were my forte, so that was a natural place to develop my niche. Fortunately, investors at the time were receptive to options because they were inexpensive.

I soon became the options coordinator for the office. The only problem was that for every new account I opened, I blew one up. Options were time bombs that exploded once a month on expiration day. It took a while for me to realize that options didn't behave like stocks. The probability of success was very low but the interest in them was very high.

I remember when, in my first year of business, a great broker named A. B. Jones said to me, "Tom, there's one way to make money in the stock market." I said, "How's that, A. B.?," and he said, "Slowly." I began to understand. Constant trading is romantic and filled with excitement, but it can be deadly. After that conversation with A. B. Jones my business turned around. I began to do more covered writing and much less trading. Most importantly, I began making money for my clients, and my book began to grow.

In June 1978 a man named Bill Walker offered me an opportunity to leave Merrill to come across the street to Wheat, First Securities to develop their first Options Strategy Department. It was a deal I could not refuse, so I left Merrill to develop my business in this new direction. About a year later, Marshall Wishnack, the head of Research at Wheat, split the Options Department into two divisions. Bill Walker ran the Options Execution Department, and I was to develop a separate Options Strategy Department to generate strategy ideas for Wheat's 500 brokers.

> *". . . most investors had just been wiped out in the bear market of 1973–74. We were prospecting leads who didn't even want to hear the word* stockbroker. *I can't tell you how many hundreds of phones were slammed on me. "*

THOMAS DORSEY

Marshall gave me an open checkbook to do what I needed to develop this state-of-the-art department. I sat alone that first week thinking how I would develop the group. I knew that if I were to be successful in this endeavor, I would have to be totally self-contained. In other words, I would have to do all my own research, make the recommendations to the brokers, and follow up on those recommendations. I asked myself a question that week: "Tom, what do you really know about stock selection and management?" The answer was a resounding, "Nothing." I had spent my brief time at Merrill taking the company's recommendations, not my own. I never developed my own way of researching; Merrill did it all for me. I looked for research help.

I searched Wheat, First high and low, talking to branch managers and veteran brokers. One name kept popping up: Steve Kane. Steve was a broker in our Charlotte, North Carolina, branch. I called him to discuss my new endeavor, and he signed on with our group. Steve's method of research was Point and Figure analysis. He had been using it for quite some time and was an expert. He showed me a little red and white paperback book written in the 1950s by A. W. Cohen called *The Three Point Reversal Method of Point and Figure Technical Analysis.*

The book helped me finally grasp the mechanics of the market. I discovered that it was supply and demand that caused price movement in the stock market. I realized that if there were more buyers than sellers willing to sell a stock, its price would rise. Conversely, if there were more sellers than buyers willing to buy, the price would decline, and if buying and selling were equal the price would stay the same. The Point and Figure method was simply a logical, organized system that recorded the movement of a stock.

After this revelation, there was no need to search any further for a way to build my options business. What made this approach so clear to me was that I saw it from the perspective of a stockbroker who had done it all wrong in the past. I had operated without a plan of action or investment strategy. When I looked back at Merrill and other competing firms, I realized that most brokers, like me, had no plan. Everyone simply took the recommendations that came down from New York and prayed they would work. Some were great, and others were dismal. It was hit or miss.

If I had had the Point and Figure method when I first started out as a broker, my clients would have fared better, and I would have had more confidence to effectively handle accounts. I knew without a doubt that if this method could transform my business, it would also transform any other broker's business. There was something so right about a method that had stood the test of time. Created by the first editor of *The Wall Street Journal,* Charles Dow, clearly it wasn't a fly-by-night strategy. I knew that this method would carry me through my career.

Steve Kane stayed with me for a year and then was off to New York to become a trader for a specialist firm on the New York Stock

Exchange. Watson Wright replaced Steve around 1981, and we have been partners in business ever since.

Although our method of analysis is the Point and Figure methodology, we have also used a system created by the late—and I must add, great—Jim Yates. His method was based on statistical analysis, the only other method I consider valid. There are many methods of technical analysis that work well in the right hands, but all I need is supply & demand and basic statistical analysis coupled with good fundamental analysis.

Watson and I resigned from Wheat and started Dorsey, Wright & Associates in 1987. At first we were simply going down the street to relocate the laboratory we had created at Wheat. Our intention was to develop the first true outsourced options strategy firm on Wall Street. I knew that many of the regional firms had Option Department heads who wore so many hats they barely had time to contemplate strategy. Their budgets didn't allow for a staff of analysts producing ideas for their brokers. We wanted to create a firm that filled that niche.

We picked up enough customers that first year to provide a salary for Watson and myself. So, as far as we were concerned, we had made it. But the crash of 1987 changed the complexion of the option business forever. We immediately put the option part of our business to the rear and brought Point and Figure analysis to the forefront. From October 1987 on we have been known as a technical analysis firm.

One of our early clients, J. C. Bradford, a wonderful southern regional firm, signed on with us to take our research firm-wide. John Felber, a partner who was in charge of the Options Strategy Department, commissioned me to travel with him to all regions of the firm to teach Point and Figure. The response was overwhelmingly positive. BT Alex. Brown, the oldest brokerage firm in the United States, soon became a client. Steve Mitchell, a partner in charge of the Options Strategy Department, commissioned me to teach the strategy to all of their brokers. Suddenly, it seemed we were in demand.

Learning to apply the Point and Figure method of analysis, combined with their own firms' fundamental research, gave our clients an organized method for managing their business—and one that set them apart from their competitors. As I had discovered in my early college days, the key to success is confidence in what you are doing, and these brokers were gaining that confidence.

After spending the first twelve months traveling and teaching, one account lead to another. Today we advise over 250 broker-dealers and numerous money managers throughout the world. We provide daily research on the world markets as well as a total charting and portfolio system over the Internet at www.dorsey wright.com. We also have a money management arm in California where our portfolio managers use this method, coupled with fundamentals, to manage individual portfolios on a discretionary basis.

> *". . .a great broker named A. B. Jones said to me, 'Tom, there's one way to make money in the stock market.' I said, 'How's that, A. B?,' and he said, 'Slowly.'"*

THOMAS DORSEY

I had always wanted to start a stockbroker institute to teach this method on a more formal basis. It finally materialized in 1992, and we now hold at least three courses a year that are oversubscribed in one day and carry a long waiting list. Our business has been expanding at 35 percent per year since we started, and it has grown primarily by word of mouth.

But even with the information and expertise that we provide, we are constantly reassessing and restructuring our services to meet evolving market needs. The investment terrain is changing rapidly with the advent of the Internet. What was once proprietary to the brokerage industry is now free on the Internet. The full-service stockbroker used to be the only game in town; now he has become the most expensive method a firm has for delivering its products to

the public. One can only guess what the next five years will bring—
or the next twenty.

This chapter presented my story in order to serve as a preamble
to the rest of the book. I've shared some of my experiences with
prospecting, building a business, partnering, developing an investment strategy, finding a niche, and adapting to business needs.
The segments that follow address these and other major issues
that I have encountered over the years, issues that I've found vital
to compete as a broker. I've interviewed some of the top people in
this industry in order to capture a wide array of experiences and
perspectives.

I hope that through these candid conversations you will better
understand the complexities faced by brokers today and formulate
a competitive game plan—such a plan is essential in an age in
which the financial services industry is changing and evolving
almost daily.

CHAPTER 2

THE ART OF PROSPECTING

PROSPECTING IS ARGUABLY the most difficult part of a stockbroker's day. Phoning people you have never met is an exceptionally difficult task. I happen to be one of those people who was born to sell, but prospecting came tough even to me. It was a love/hate kind of thing: I knew the possibility of opening a really big account was always there on the other end of the phone, but I also knew the probability was slim.

To succeed in this difficult part of the business, one must learn to accept rejection. It comes down to work ethic. For every hundred prospecting calls you make, there will be only a small percentage who are receptive. That percentage is low, but if you dial enough numbers you will open new accounts. It's a simple game of numbers and chance.

One of the most successful prospectors I have ever met is Jim DeMent, who is interviewed in Chapter 3 about relationship building. Jim was a broker at Merrill Lynch when I started in the business. He had an incredibly effective, yet simple, strategy for generating business: he made a game out of it. Each day he would phone ten people he had never talked to before. He would then add those ten to the accumulated number to date and continue on. If for whatever reason he did not contact ten new people in a day, he would have to erase his total and go back to zero.

I watched him dial religiously. Although I was amazed at his perseverance and the results his work generated, I never adopted the program myself. I was too interested in doing the production of the day rather than prospecting. If I were back on the production line I would surely be implementing Jim's program. The numbers really add up. Ten people a day, times twenty days a month, you have talked to 200 new people. If only 3 percent become customers, then you have opened six new accounts in a month.

Calling is not the only method of prospecting, however. Seminars, too, can be a very fruitful strategy, but only if you have something valuable to say. Seminars offer the opportunity to get your message across to a large group of people, rather than to one person at a time on the phone.

When I started as a broker, seminars were one of my main methods of prospecting. But I was incredibly nervous the first time I stood up in front of a group. I was able to conquer that giant fear, however, by greeting each person entering the room. I tried to create small talk, so that by the time I started the seminar, I was at ease with the group. It's a method that has worked for me.

I speak at least forty times a year now and over the past ten years have held hundreds of seminars on technical analysis. Successful public speaking comes from within. The reason I am able to hold a crowd's attention is because I believe in what I am saying and I say it with enthusiasm. I also have a sincere desire to share knowledge with others.

If you are not a natural public speaker, there are ways to improve any presentation. Think for a moment about what you are truly passionate about. Maybe it's antique cars, possibly golf. Whatever the topic, you will give a far better speech (or sales pitch) if you are talking about your favorite subject.

That passion for the subject, combined with true confidence, will help set you apart from the thousands of other brokers and planners who are competing for business. I am often prospected by cold callers who have absolutely nothing to say except that their firm "has great stock picks." Well, every investor has heard that same line from a dozen different brokers—it isn't a message that will distinguish anyone from the rest of the pack. I could call brokers in town to get their best stock recommendations. What added value is the caller bringing to the table? The answer is: absolutely none.

To retain your current base of clients and attract more you must bring something more to the table than everyone else. Now, let's move on to how two of the best in the business go about attracting and keeping individual and institutional clients.

INTERVIEW

Laurence C. Pettit, III, Scott & Stringfellow, Inc. Richmond, Virginia

LARRY PETTIT IS ONE of the most effective prospectors I know. One of the things that prompted me to interview Larry for this book is his use of S-curves in his prospecting endeavors. Larry uses a creative approach that has won him a lot of new business.

This concept of the "S-curve" is something I had studied and become fascinated with when I read the book *Predictions*, written by Theodore Modis, a Greek physicist living and working in Switzerland. He is a man who has an answer to any question you might pose.

His book opened my mind to new concepts. For instance, did you know that the average speed for an automobile is still 30 miles per hour and has not changed since the first Model T came off the assembly line? We now have muscle cars capable of 180 miles per hour right out of the factory, but we also have many more impediments to speed, like stop signs, stoplights, and traffic jams, that hold the average speed down to 30 miles per hour. It is also interesting to note that we as humans walk at an average speed of 3 miles per hour, the average car travels at 30 miles per hour, and the average aircraft travels at 300 miles per hour. Would this suggest the next generation of aircraft will travel at 3,000 miles per hour? Food for thought.

I also learned from his book that the average number of deaths per 100,000 drivers has only fluctuated between 22 and 26 since the inception of the first motorized auto. One hundred years ago there was no such thing as seatbelts, children's safety seats, and other safety equipment. Today, every sort of safety device is required in all cars, yet the same number of deaths occurs. When the average number of deaths reached 22 per 100M the government raised the speed limit from 55 to 75 in some states. This has had the effect of ratcheting the average number of deaths back up to the 26 per 100M level. My guess is when 26 is hit again, the government will require us to wear crash helmets in autos. As Professor Modis states in his book, "Once a natural growth process has been established, its future course is predictable." He uses S-curves to chart that process.

This is where Larry takes his prospects. He applies the S-curve to investment needs by discussing just where a potential investor might be on his natural growth curve. During the first meeting he gets his prospects thinking about where they are on their life's S-curve. This in turn helps them come to grips with which investments will be needed to provide for their retirement. Larry says it's an eye-opening approach for all classes of investors from smaller accounts to CFOs of major corporations. It's a unique perspective that offers his clients a compelling starting point.

When I was waiting for Larry to arrive for our meeting I asked one of his fellow brokers what he knew about Larry. His response was, with a smile, "He's a machine."

TOM DORSEY: I think your story and your methods will be of real interest to other brokers. Let's begin with how you started in this business.

LARRY PETTIT: I finally realized I wanted to be a stockbroker when I was thirty. I had been in the business at a much younger age, then out of the business, knowing that I didn't have enough maturity to be there. When I came back it was with a totally different attitude. I wanted to work for a friendly firm that everybody in the community knows and trusts, so I joined Scott & Stringfellow. I've been there for seven years now, and during that time I've developed one of the fastest-growing businesses at my firm.

DORSEY: Your branch manager, Jordan Ball, has said that you are the best in the firm at developing new business. Tell me how you've learned to do that.

PETTIT: My father is a finance professor at the University of Virginia, so for the first eighteen or twenty years of my life all I heard about was finance. Some of this information ultimately sank in. After I had started as a broker, my father came to Richmond and took me to lunch. He turned over a napkin in that restaurant, and he drew an S-curve. He said, "Everything you need to know is on this curve." The standard deviation of the market ultimately derives from this curve as well as the product life cycle, he explained. And from that curve I have developed my business. This is the central concept I use to develop my business. I get out and meet people, but I educate them on that S-curve model using a teaching tool that I have developed. It works because it allows all investors large or small to see the big picture.

DORSEY: Tell me about the mechanics of how you generate business. You've been called a machine. Why?

PETTIT: In essence, I get in front of as many people as I can. I try to get to know my customers and put myself in their shoes. The one thing I think we as brokers don't do well is relate to our clients. We really don't think about what they are going through at the various stages in their lives. When I see a client, I expect to learn his whole financial condition. I accomplish this by a teaching strategy I developed to succinctly explain what the product life is. By the time I leave, I'm going to know everything he has, and I've taught the product life cycle theory.

> ## *"The one thing I think we as brokers don't do well is relate to our clients. We really don't think about what they are going through at the various stages in their lives. "*
>
> ### LARRY PETTIT

DORSEY: So you relate the prospect's financial position in life to the product life cycle or the S-curve?

PETTIT: Right, I help them understand where they are on their own financial S-curve. Everything relates to the product life cycle.

DORSEY: Walk me through the process you use when meeting with prospective clients.

PETTIT: I use Circuit City as one example; it's a big name in Richmond, Virginia. From 1986 to 1993 it was one of the top five performing stocks on the New York Stock Exchange. I relate Circuit City's life cycle to that of the prospect I'm talking to. These people all know the story of Circuit City. They've probably shopped there for many years.

In 1987 Circuit City was operating mostly in cities in the southeast. By 1993 it had reached the apex; it was in almost every major market in America. Common sense would tell you that the growth curve in this particular stock was going to slow down, because in evaluating a retail stock, half the story is same-store sales; the other half of the story is store growth. So I relate this story to individuals in our community. They are fascinated by it because they see it every day. They don't fully understand it, but they see it. I carry the customer through that cycle and ask: "Where do you think Circuit City is today?" I ask them to try to pinpoint where Circuit City is on the curve. I then explain that the low side would carry the highest potential return but also the highest risk. The top end of the curve would represent the least amount of potential return but the lowest risk.

DORSEY: Do you have a way of demonstrating that on paper at the first meeting? Do you actually show the S-curve?

PETTIT: I draw it. I go through a complete training seminar that's very simple and quick. I also use IBM as an example because it carries through several different products that everyone can relate to. This was a company that once developed manual typewriters, and its typewriter was the lead product, until the electric typewriter came in. As each product in the company matured, the company had to make a decision about what kind of product would come next. In IBM's case, the mainframe computer succeeded the electronic typewriter, and then mainframes reached the top of the S-curve. Rather than operate at the top of its S-curve and risk falling suddenly, IBM went back to the low end of the S-curve and developed the PC market. I use the same stocks over and over again, because they are easy to remember and it usually makes sense to the investor. I carry an HP 12C programmable calculator with me at all times. When the customer identifies where he thinks he is on the curve, I can simply ask how much money he has. Now, if he tells me, I can tell him what he will need to have in liquid assets in five, ten, or twenty years. This method allows me to get a financial profile on the client without being impersonal.

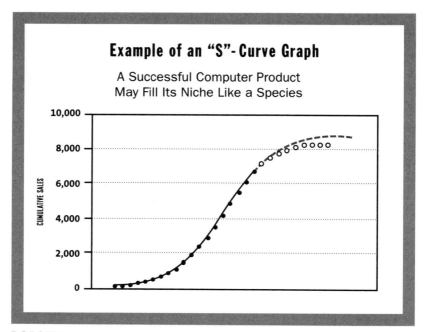

Example of an "S"-Curve Graph

A Successful Computer Product May Fill Its Niche Like a Species

SOURCE: USED WITH PERMISSION FROM *PREDICTIONS*, BY THEODORE MODIS, PH.D.

DORSEY: Let's discuss how you get the prospect to understand risk relative to his own S-curve.

PETTIT: I ask the investor, "If risk were not a consideration, and you could make an investment of $10,000 in Door A or Door B, and Door A is going to be worth $100,000 in ten years and Door B is going to be worth half a million, which door would you pick?" They all pick Door B. But the reality of the matter is that in order to get high returns, there is going to be much greater risk. The reason is, the client is going to have to place himself way down on the curve. Think about the curve again. The bottom half carries the biggest possibility of gain but it also carries the highest risk. The client's life is now on the upper side of the curve. He will either have to place more money in at the lower risk level, or he must put the same amount in at the lower end of the curve, but in a much riskier investment. This is where the client must deal with the risks that he is willing to take to reach his goals. I use a model to demonstrate potential returns after taxes and inflation to help the client pinpoint his goal.

DORSEY: OK, Larry, here is a case in point. I opened an account for my children the day they were born and bought them some stock. My oldest is 18 now, and eighteen years ago I did not have much money to invest. I bought him about $600 worth of both Coca-Cola and Alcoa—a small amount of money at the exact start of his S-curve. My investment was low, but the risk was high because I only had enough to invest in two stocks. It is now exactly eighteen years later and that $600 is worth $24,000. He is still very low on his S-curve so I have opened an IRA for him now because he works at Pizza Hut as a pizza cutter. Not a glamorous job, but when he is 45 my guess is he will be able to retire because I have him thinking and planning for his retirement while he is on the lower end of his curve.

Let's talk about the curve for a second. Our prospective client says, "Okay, I'm ready to move forward." Where do you go with the interview now?

PETTIT: If the client is ready to move forward, we have to find out exactly what risks he needs to take to arrive at his goal. It may be that he can't afford to take any risk at all. The first thing I need to know is how much he makes now. Suppose he makes $60,000 a year, has worked for Philip Morris for twenty-five years, is married with two children just out of college, and owns a house on which he only owes $20,000.

Next, I will ask about liquid assets, such as the 401(k) at Philip Morris. Suppose he has $200,000 in that and has taken a lot of vacations along the way, so he doesn't have much in savings. Just by answering a few simple questions, he has given me the whole profile, without any pushing.

DORSEY: Now that you have that information, how do you determine what his risk is?

PETTIT: I then pull out my calculator and figure out, based on today's dollars, what it's going to take for him to retire. I think it's best to give him the answer to his question during this meeting. I just did this last week, and the gentleman I went to see had also visited an American Express planner. The planner came out and got all the information, and said, "I've got to go back to my office and I'll send you the results." But I was able to give him the numbers right there. Finally, I want to know if the client plans to make any lifestyle changes when he retires. Most prospects want to have at least their present salary. Let's calculate what he'll need to retire on in seventeen years at 65, assuming he is 48 now.

> *"The ultimate goal of the market plan is to create a self-sustaining feeder network for my business. As my business grows, the efficiency of this marketing plan plays a larger role."*
>
> LARRY PETTIT

There are lots of options that can help people save money, such as refinancing the house and pulling some of the cash out of it. If you add that to the $200,000, that debt might be eradicated in fifteen years, and you would have a lot more money if you were willing to risk a little bit. Maybe we can add a monthly investment program. It looks to me like there is another $150 a month lying around. What we really need to do is develop a plan and stick to it, because once I know the story I can really help him execute it. By then you the broker are walking out with the check. You've just signed another client.

DORSEY: You have reached the top of your S-curve.

PETTIT: The sales presentation is right at the top of its S-curve. And you know what's great about it? I've been able to help someone out. That's what it's all about. So few brokers ask the right questions to accomplish this. Most of them are just selling the next stock that comes down the pike from research. Even the most sophisticated investor can learn something from this presentation. They generally haven't thought about where they are on their own S-curve.

DORSEY: How do you get the people to contact to begin with?

PETTIT: I use a marketing plan that I call "full court press." I market myself continually through all of my contacts. I get involved in the community and try to add value to whatever I bring to the customer. I'll try to give you a few examples here.

I have a corporate client who owns the fastest growing company in Richmond. I've been with this gentleman from day one. I have helped him get his financial statements in order, obtain working capital, and take care of his personal finances. By getting involved in the company, many of the employees have become clients.

All people I meet are potential customers, and I want them to call me when they have any kind of financial dilemma. These calls help me develop a financial referral network. If I have a client who needs a mortgage I can refer him to a mortgage banker or an accountant. This network is part of my full court press marketing plan and the referrals come back to me many times over. The ultimate goal of the market plan is to create a self-sustaining feeder network for my business. As my business grows, the efficiency of this marketing plan plays a larger role.

DORSEY: How involved do you get in your clients' financial lives?

PETTIT: I try to be involved in every financial decision my clients make. I don't want them to do anything without talking to me, because I might be able to help them. It's not that I want to get into their private business, it's just that I know a lot of people who may be able to help my clients. That keeps me in the loop with their whole financial situation.

I'm out looking for the next client. I'm always working; even when I'm on the road I'm making calls to my clients. My sales assistant and I are always thinking about where we are on our S-curve, where we want to be in a year, and what the slope of the curve is going to be.

DORSEY: Are you capable of mathematically creating an S-curve of where you are?

PETTIT: Yes, I do it every day. If I don't know where I am on the curve, how will I know how hard I need to work to maintain my current business or expand it? I use a production growth model to help me do my planning. The production growth model helps me identify how many new assets I need to attract during the year to meet the production goals I set for myself. The Production Growth Model is calculated by using the following formula.

A Assets under Management x Return on Assets = Expected Production

B Production Goal - Expected Production = Production Shortfall

C Production Shortfall / Expected Return on Assets = Assets Needed to Accumulate

It's very simple, and I can calculate it on a monthly basis. So that growth model is letting me know where I stand and how hard I need to be working if I want to meet my goals.

Lets go through an example to practically apply this model.

1998 Production:	$600,000
1999 Goal:	$750,000
A.U.M. 12/31/98:	$35,000,000
ROA in 1998:	1.5%

A 35,000,000 X .015 = $525,000 Expected Production

B $750,000 - $525,000 = $225,000 Production Shortfall

C $225,000 / 2.5% = $9,000,000 Assets Needed to Accumulate

$9,000,000 is amount of assets needed to meet 1999 production goals.

Many of these applications could be used to establish and track trends at the brokerage houses. I believe that production life cycle and production growth model can be crucial tools in helping brokerage firms manage at the retail level. I have not built any historical models but I believe a firm could develop these models and they may ultimately help senior management make planning decisions.

> *"A rookie should be out of the office meeting people as much as possible. Every telephone contact should lead to a face-to-face meeting."*
>
> LARRY PETTIT

DORSEY: You have opened a lot of accounts over the past five years. How do you think your S-curve model applies to rookie brokers?

PETTIT: Just like a start-up corporation, a rookie broker is going to have certain tasks that he wants to accomplish that will lay the groundwork for his career. A rookie should be out of the office meeting people as much as possible. Every telephone contact should lead to a face-to-face meeting. You might call this Phase One.

The job is fairly simple at this stage. You should try to extend Phase One as long as you can. The focus should be on opening accounts. The rookie broker should keep things simple, especially when it comes to the product. Certain types of investments take a lot more time than others. So, if you have clients who want to own more complicated investments, you might not have the time to continue to get out and see clients because you'll feel obligated to sit at your desk and track the complex investments.

As you move into Phase Two, the job branches out and gets fairly complex. You become a juggler. You become a marketer, an asset manager, and a planner. If you can make the transition into Phase Two and still get out to see new clients, you have a chance to extend your growth model. This is the toughest phase in the development of a brokerage career.

As your schedule gets more complicated, you may have to make changes in order to continue to grow. So knowing when you are approaching this critical point could have a huge impact on your long-term production growth rate.

"What is going to keep the broker alive in the 21st century is taking care of his client's interests in a professional manner and having the knowledge and ability to understand the stock markets. "

LARRY PETTIT

DORSEY: So would you say task management is critical to the long-term success of a broker?

PETTIT: Yes. I think that education and employee seminars are critical at this phase of your career. Those seminars ultimately help you with task management. Mastering each task is important, so you have to know what those tasks are—marketing, administrating, managing, educating (both yourself and your clients), and planning. If you can master these tasks then you should be able to continue to open accounts and increase your assets under management. Naturally, work ethic plays a large role in it.

DORSEY: So the S-curve can be broken up into phases and ultimately into multi-tasking. What about the Production Growth Model?

PETTIT: I use that model to set the stage for where I want to be next year. So when you are planning for the next calendar year, the first thing you have to do is calculate how much you need to increase your assets under management in order to meet your production goal. Then you use the other task management process to help you reach those goals. This is a macro viewpoint for being a successful broker. There are many specific actions that work well. That is what makes the brokerage industry so interesting.

DORSEY: Larry, thanks for taking the time to let me interview you. What thought would you like to leave the reader with?

PETTIT: What is going to keep the broker alive in the 21st century is taking care of his client's interests in a professional manner and having the knowledge and ability to understand the stock markets. My own personal system, using S-curve, is my way of achieving this.

LAURENCE C. PETTIT, III is employed as a First Vice President at Scott & Stringfellow in Richmond, Virginia. Mr. Pettit is a graduate of Mary Washington College and has been an active participant in the investment industry for fifteen years. Mr. Pettit has been with Scott & Stringfellow since 1991. In addition to the securities industry, Mr. Pettit has been involved in both the real estate and the venture capital industries.

Neile Wolfe, Prudential Securities Incorporated Austin, Texas

MY PARTNER WATSON WRIGHT recommended that I interview Neile Wolfe for this section. Watson met him at a country club in Austin, Texas, and was impressed with how he is able to sign large corporate option plans. Like many young brokers, I took the rifle approach to prospecting. I typically called people who made less money than I did. But Neile bypasses the individual investor and goes right to the corporate level. Capturing a large customer like this can carry a broker a long way. It takes a lot of individual clients to equal one corporate pension plan or stock option program. Neile has found a way to build this into his business and outlines it for us here.

TOM DORSEY: Let's talk about how you started in this business.

NEILE WOLFE: I started as a broker in 1980. That was a time when people still walked through the doors seeking advice from brokers. For the first ten years of my career, I was pretty lackadaisical because I didn't need to make very much money. Everything I had was paid for, and so I simply worked enough to get by and was generally a goof-off. But when I got married and we had our first child, my wife wanted to stay home with the baby, so I realized that I needed to increase my income. I always hated prospecting, so I needed to find a way to make the process of opening accounts easier.

In Austin, there were some technology companies that were granting stock options to their employees. So I went around to the technology companies and asked if there was some way that I could help employees to exercise those stock options. It is a really cumbersome process, which they needed to streamline, so they offered to make me the preferred vendor for their stock options.

I spent about a week with the company and went through all

the steps, and came up with a pretty novel idea: the Options Department no longer had to be in a paper environment; it could be in an electronic environment by using e-mail. That company just happened to be Dell Computer Corporation.

DORSEY: What a client! That is a major home run.

WOLFE: As a result, I was the number one account opener in Prudential Securities for about three years running. One year my assistant and I opened close to 2,000 accounts. And all the account applications came in over e-mail. So not only was I free of the process of prospecting, I was getting paid because everybody who opened an account sold either their employee stock purchase shares or their stock options through me.

With all of this money flowing through the accounts, I thought that some of these people would like to reinvest the proceeds. So we decided to ask everyone who had more than $250,000 left over after their option exercise if they would like to sit in and do some financial planning. A number of them agreed, so we started capturing most of the proceeds from the option exercise.

DORSEY: Is Dell the only firm that you work with now on the stock options program?

WOLFE: Curiously enough, the turnover at Dell was such that in a six-year period, I had to deal with four different vice presidents of Human Resources, and I finally lost the Dell account in the summer of 1996. But since I had done this once, it was easy for me to do it again. So this time I put together three other brokers, and we made it our business focus to prospect for the 401(k) plans and stock option plans of technology companies.

DORSEY: How much money do you oversee?

WOLFE: I have about 400 clients and a $400 million book, so my average account size is $1 million, and my median account size is probably $400,000 to $500,000. When you have a book that big, it's impossible to trade the book, so I have had to modify the Dorsey, Wright system. I cannot get around and call everybody fast enough to be in and out of client meetings as frequently as the Dorsey, Wright model might suggest I do when a stock breaks down below its upward trend line. I would have to make 400 phone calls to get people in my office.

I have always preferred the buy-and-hold model, so I made a list of what I considered to be the 200 best companies in the world, companies that are going to be here thirty-five and forty years in the future. Even if these companies go through a very difficult period, they will come out on top.

DORSEY: I assume you are talking about the old adage of buying the stocks when they are low?

WOLFE: Yes. Every week, I go through the Point and Figure charts of all 200 companies to check the industry sector and the sector bullish percentages. When I find that there is a particular industry that has been thoroughly decimated, the whole industry is down, and the sector bullish percentage is below 30, then I start paying particular attention to the Point and Figure charts of the major players in that industry.

For instance, when the semiconductor stocks get trashed, I want to take a look at the industry leaders within that particular category. I go take a look at Intel, Applied Materials, and Novellus Systems. Once I see that the sector is starting to reverse up from below 30 percent, and the Point and Figure charts appear to be reversing up, then I'll go to all my clients and buy stocks in that particular industry sector with the expectation that they will still own them ten or fifteen years from now. Then I'll wait for the next industry sector to be thoroughly trashed and will make substantial purchases in that industry sector.

Occasionally, I will decide that I want to lighten up in an industry sector, as I have been doing so recently in the banking industry. We have had a multi-year period where we've had the bullish percentage above 70 percent, we have had huge moves in the stocks, and we are starting to see some breakdown in the industry bullish percentage. I really don't want to completely sell my clients out of Citicorp entirely, but I think reducing their exposure here makes some sense. I manage the purchase of the inventory using sector bullish percentages, concentrating on the three or four world-class companies within that sector and buying them with the idea that my clients will hold them permanently.

DORSEY: Do you corner the accounts with anything like the spiders or the Dogs of the Dow or the Relative Strength Five, or does your strategy use strictly a portfolio of equities? Do you use a bond ladder?

WOLFE: Yes, I do both individual treasuries and individual junk bonds, as an income complement to those people who need income. A typical account I manage would have some exposure to fixed income, but it is using the Dow Jones Bond Average for entry and exit points. It is a methodical and thorough approach. My clients have done exceptionally well, but there have been times when they probably could have picked up some extra return if I had been willing to trade out of a position.

DORSEY: How do you explain your investment strategy to your clients?

WOLFE: The very first thing that I do is put together a plan: What do you have? Where do you want to be? How are you going to get there? This helps me to understand what their portfolios should look like. Some of the Dell employees who are retiring in their mid-thirties don't have a portfolio that looks like that of a typical mid-thirty-year-old. They are walking out of Dell with $3 million to $5 million, and they are out of the labor force. So their portfolio looks substantially different than somebody's who is thirty years old and is still in the capital accumulation phase.

Then I explain to them that my investment methodology involves buying sectors of the stock market that are out of favor. I buy only the highest quality companies in that sector and hold onto them for long periods of time. I explain to them that at some point in the future, we will talk about the actual methodology that I use to buy into the sectors. It might be three or four years down the road. They just want a clear, unequivocal statement that I have an investment methodology that is based on their needs.

DORSEY: Do you find many do-it-yourselfers now? What is your take on the Internet and what that technology has provided to customers and prospects?

WOLFE: I really don't see the Internet as competition. I think that the Internet segregates the client base. A lot of people are disinterested in running their own financial portfolio on a day-to-day basis. It allows market stratification that wasn't possible before, but there are still a substantial number of people who don't have any real interest in the actual mechanics of running a portfolio.

DORSEY: Did you have any problems at all with customers wanting discounts because they see on television that they can trade for $5?

WOLFE: I have discounted for a long period of time, and certainly I don't charge full rates. But I don't have any people complaining about the commission rate.

DORSEY: Why don't you charge full commissions? With what you are doing, it seems to me it is well worth full commissions.

WOLFE: Well, you know, my typical commissions average about 1 percent. I feel that 1 percent is a reasonable portfolio management rate.

DORSEY: What do you think about portfolio management, as a business? I can tell you, after a market crash they won't be too happy to pay a fee for the broker who is losing their money.

WOLFE: I think the whole wrap fee business is going to have a difficult time. The whole idea about wrapping an account is really great in a rising market, but it comes apart in a falling market. Clients see their account drop three or six quarters in a row, and they are going to ask why they are paying this money to watch their account go down.

I truly believe that the entire wrap fee process will be substantially different once we go through the next bear market. As a commissioned broker, I am never going to blow my book up, and people understand that I have a methodology.

"...my investment methodology involves buying sectors of the stock market that are out of favor. I buy only the highest quality companies in that sector, and hold onto them for long periods of time."

NEILE WOLFE

DORSEY: How is your confidence level today compared to ten years ago?

WOLFE: There is no comparison. I was like Moses wandering in the desert searching for the Promised Land, and now I feel like I've found it.

DORSEY: Tell me what your long-term goals are as they relate to prospecting.

WOLFE: My long-term goal is to have a billion-dollar book and be doing $2,500,000 in production. I don't think that my billion-dollar target is too high based upon the way the methodology that I use garners assets and the way I manage money.

DORSEY: But what would you say the minimum size account would be that you could work with?

WOLFE: The smallest account that I take now is $500,000, and I'll probably take that up to a million dollars. What I do now is take my smaller-sized accounts and pass them on to the other three people on my team because they can give them service I am hard pressed to do right now.

DORSEY: Will they follow along with the same concept then?

WOLFE: Yes. They are slowly adopting my methodology.

DORSEY: Talking to you, Neile, almost makes me want to go back into production.

WOLFE: I've developed something that really works for us. We have gone into a company to set up the 401(k) plan; we have all of the founders of the company as individual clients; and when the company goes public, the founders alone should bring in probably 250 million dollars' worth of founders stock. And that founders stock will eventually be transferred to other assets.

By the time we have fifteen to twenty-five companies (pre-public, venture-capital, venture-technology companies), each one of us could be approaching a billion dollars in assets-under-management. So, we recognized that we need to have a planning relationship with these clients and the sophistication to deal with their investment needs. And in doing so, it was vital to use an investment methodology that allowed us that sophistication, and Point and Figure charts seemed to be the way to do it. Having the methodology is paramount to building the business. It should be built into the plan. I could have spent the rest of my brokerage career fumbling around for the right tools to be a value-added service had I not discovered Point and Figure. It's one of the things that has allowed me to develop a methodology that was true value-added for my clients. That's what builds a broker's business.

NEILE WOLFE, who has over 400 clients in twenty states, serves as Senior Vice President of Investments for Prudential Securities. Having been with Prudential Securities for eighteen years, he is a member of the President's Council and the Prudential Investments 401(k) Advisory Council, and was ranked tenth for assets under management at Prudential in 1998. Wolfe's other activities include being President of the Austin Chapter of the National Association of Stock Plan Professionals; serving on the Board of Directors of Ambion, Inc., an Austin, Texas, biotechnology firm; and being an angel investor for four other Austin technology start-up firms.

CHAPTER 3

BUILDING RELATIONSHIPS

RELATIONSHIP BUILDING IS one of the most important
tasks for brokers. It's an art more subtle than prospecting—but no less important. Rule 405 NYSE (the guide-
line that applies to knowing your customer) comes into
play *after* the prospect becomes a customer. It entails
finding out exactly what your customer is trying to attain
with his investment endeavors. It's a process of asking
the right questions, delving into your customer's back-

ground, determining tolerance for risk, and knowing whether he is focused on the short or long term.

When I was a stockbroker, I had clients ranging from the wildest speculators to the most conservative utility stock buyers. Every broker is faced with the same dilemma: each customer has very different needs. Some firms today try to deal with this by programming the answers to a few key questions into a computer that prints an instant financial plan. But building a relationship requires you go much deeper than a one-size-fits-all computer spreadsheet.

What makes effective relationship building particularly difficult is that some customers don't have a clear understanding of what their financial goals are. Others do know what they need, but have difficulty communicating their wishes. I've had many customers tell me that their interest was primarily in trading. They expressed a desire to catch short-term market swings or to trade on margin. If I had probed deeper, however, I would have found that many of these people were really long-term investors saving for retirement. Like many brokers, I didn't ask the right questions. Creating an integrated plan for their future is one of the ways to keep their business and build on it with referrals.

A gentleman approached me after a recent seminar I gave in Minnesota. He was dissatisfied with the performance of a mutual fund because it wasn't keeping pace with the S&P 500. I explained to him that in order to outperform the S&P 500 (at this time), his fund would have had to be continually invested in the top forty stocks in the S&P with an overweighting on high technology. But after talking to this gentleman, I found that he was not interested in making a large bet in technology; the volatility was too high for this stage of his life.

Our conversation made him feel more comfortable with his fund because he realized that it had given him a very reasonable return with relatively low volatility. Assisting clients with financial planning and helping them understand their needs is all part of a broker's job today. Being involved in your customer's financial education will surely benefit the longevity and richness of the relationship.

Another benefit of getting to know your clients is recognizing when you need to fire them. The moment that you learn that your services are a poor fit with their needs or that they are being dishonest about their goals and motives, it's time to consider cutting them loose.

I once had a dilemma with a client who knew more about option margins than I did. To make matters worse, his accounts were cross-margined, making any margin calculation a nightmare. I should have fired this guy when I realized he was more interested in stretching the rules than in sensible investing. Over a period of time I lost a tremendous amount of sleep over this account, but eventually chose to keep the client because of the commissions he generated. Big mistake. That decision led to a close call with the FBI.

> *"Being involved in your customer's financial education will surely benefit the longevity and richness of the relationship."*
>
> THOMAS DORSEY

It turned out that my client had broken the law without my even realizing it. He had taken out a loan at an Elizabeth City bank and used Georgia Pacific bonds as collateral. Sometime later, he contacted the Georgia Pacific transfer agent and told him the bonds had been burned up in a fire. I, however, had no idea the bonds had been replaced by the transfer agent. The customer then sold the replacement bonds through me. At the time I had no knowledge of the Elizabeth City connection. The bonds came signed by him and in good order. I sold them and mailed out the money on settlement date. At some point after that, he missed a couple of payments on the loan at the Elizabeth City bank, and the bank decided to foreclose on the loan and sell the bonds. But, of course, the bonds were no longer valid.

The FBI contacted me to find out what I knew about the situation. Of course, I only knew that he gave me an order to sell bonds and delivered them on settlement date, as he had done in every case in the past. He somehow managed to wiggle out of trouble and still I kept the account. (This is a client who could have ruined my career, and I was ready to risk it for the almighty commission!) That was my mistake. Part of building a relationship with your customers is understanding them well enough to know when to let go of the account.

All brokers have clients that cause sleepless nights, and then many others who make the business fun and interesting. The more you find out about each of your clients, the better the relationship will be. A doctor finds out everything he can about a patient's medical history before he treats him; the same principle applies to brokers. Here are some thoughts on relationship building from one of the best brokers I know.

INTERVIEW

James H. DeMent, Jr., Davenport & Company LLC Richmond, Virginia

I MET JIM THE FIRST DAY I started at Merrill back in the mid-1970s. Jim, who was already an established broker, was a role model for us rookies. Jim has been building relationships for the past twenty-four years; he is another broker I would not have a second thought about giving my family accounts to for managing. He's a solid all-around family man with the highest standards and integrity. He's also a graduate from West Point, which is apparent in his work ethic and his standards.

I remember Jim prospecting in the '70s. He was as disciplined as anyone I knew then. Most of the brokers in our office were trading-oriented. We were plain vanilla stockbrokers. We were in the business of outguessing the market. Jim's approach was always so much more thoughtful.

One of the reasons that Jim excels at relationship building is that he always asks the right questions. Week after week, Jim sat down with elderly couples to discuss their whole financial situation. And because he was willing to take the time to discuss their long-term financial plans, he ended up managing entire accounts. Most of the rookies were just dealing with the tip of the iceberg— we took whatever portion of the client's capital that we could get regardless of an overall investment plan. I think it would have scared most of us out of our wits if a wealthy individual wanted a total financial plan.

After twenty-four years, I find Jim doing the same thing that brought him success at Merrill Lynch. He is now at a Richmond, Virginia–based firm called Davenport. Jim's business has grown considerably, but curiously enough, he has never expanded his staff. He still uses one sales assistant who is shared with other brokers, and he is the broker of record. That's it. You wonder how he can develop a good-sized business and keep his staff at a minimum. Well, the answer lies in the interview, but I'll give you a preview. Jim specializes in equities and takes a long-term view of building wealth for his clients.

TOM DORSEY: It's been about twenty-four years since we first met, and you're one of the brokers I admire most. But before we get into that, tell me a little bit about how you started in the business at Merrill Lynch and how you began to develop your own business.

JIM DEMENT: I spent about ten years in the air force and started in the brokerage business in November 1972. I was hired in Richmond at Legg Mason and Company. After a year, they closed the office because a recession had started and business had dropped off. The Dow was at 1,050 the day I joined Legg Mason, and about a year-and-a-half later it was 577, with New York Stock Exchange volume at about 7 million shares a day.

That was my first year in the business. I was in a strange town, and I didn't know a soul. Somehow I managed to feed my three small daughters. After Legg Mason closed the office, I went to Merrill Lynch on the first of August '74 and was there for nineteen years. Since then, I've been at Davenport and Company LLC. for close to five years, so I've seen a lot of markets.

DORSEY: Tell me about '73–74 and what that market was like for you.

DEMENT: It was very negative, because those were the years when we were in the process of extracting ourselves from Vietnam. There was a lot of debt in the economy, and there were all sorts of problems. Nixon resigned one week after I got to Merrill Lynch, and the market had gone down 50 percent from over 1,000 to under 600, and people were avoiding it like mad. If you were just starting in the business, the only possible way to make it was to continue to look for new business, talk to as many people as possible, try to find out who would do business with you. If you helped them, they would refer to you someone who you could build a relationship with.

> *". . . as soon as brokers develop a nucleus*
>
> *of business and can begin to*
>
> *ask for referrals, prospecting is*
>
> *a whole lot easier. "*
>
> JIM DEMENT

DORSEY: Was your prospecting primarily by telephone or face-to-face? How did you prospect when the timing was the toughest in that bear market?

DEMENT: I did both. I did whatever it took to try to feed my family. I made a lot of telephone calls each day, but I also found it important to get out of the office. I once went to a major office building in downtown Richmond, the Ross Building, and I went floor by floor from top to bottom, knocking on doors and walking in and visiting people. Believe it or not, I met people who are still my clients. I did the same thing in an area called Scott's

Addition in the West End. I went to all of these businesses, handing people my card and asking if I could be of some help. And somehow I generated enough business to have about 160 or 170 clients by the time Legg Mason closed its office and I went to Merrill.

DORSEY: I have never heard anyone talk about going through a building door to door.

DEMENT: I was looking for people who might be able to do some business, and I was looking under every rock I could find. Cold calling is quite inefficient, because 95 percent of the people you talk with either have no money or no interest or both. So as soon as brokers develop a nucleus of business and can begin to ask for referrals, prospecting is a whole lot easier. I work hard for my clients and ask them to send their friends to me.

DORSEY: Tell me about the game you play to meet your prospecting quota, because it's something that I think most brokers can do to stay on track. Prospecting is a numbers game, after all.

DEMENT: Exactly right.

DORSEY: Let's go back to 1975, in the beginning.

DEMENT: In 1975, of course, I was still quite new in Richmond. When I got out of the service and we moved here, I thought it would be a nice town to live in. But I didn't have college connections, country club connections, or any of that sort of thing. I knew that in order to build a book, I was going to have to introduce myself to as many people as I could as quickly as possible. So I attempted to contact ten or more new clients every single day. You might think that doesn't add up, but over the course of a year, it's amazing. And if some of those people are then willing to refer you to their friends, things can begin to happen, even in a bad market. But the key is persistence.

DORSEY: What type of product mix do you have right now? Back in the 1970s, we were all plain vanilla stocks and bonds. How has that changed for you, or has it changed at all?

DEMENT: I'm primarily involved in equities, because over the years I have discovered that good stocks, particularly those that are bought and held for a long period of time, have the most value. I tend to buy stocks and good growth mutual funds. Most people have to struggle for the nest egg that they need for retirement. Inflation requires that the nest egg continue to grow. So that's why I encourage people to purchase stocks and growth funds and stick with them.

I have found that I don't have any ability to really trade effectively. As often as not, I'll guess incorrectly about what the market is going to do on a short-term basis. You really stack the deck in your favor when you buy good stocks over a long period of time and hold onto them while the earnings rise and the dividends go up. Even a growth stock becomes an income stock if you hold it long enough and the dividends continue to increase. That has been my approach, and it allows me to sleep at night without having to worry about the volatility in my client's portfolio.

DORSEY: Tell me about relationship building that you do so effectively with your customers.

DEMENT: Well, you learn a lot of things in a place like West Point. My training as a military officer has really helped me, because I understood what it felt like to take responsibility for other people's lives. That has carried over into the business world for me. When I meet any new prospect or client, my assumption is that this person deserves my respect, and I'm going to treat him just the way I would want him to treat me.

Once in a while you run into a client that is just not worthy of respect. These are the people that try to treat you badly. Even when I was scratching to make a living for my little kids, I let people like that go somewhere else to do business. I have a standard policy of not dealing with people like that.

In all these years I've never had one compliance problem, complaint, any sort of legal action, and I know it's because I'm very careful about NYSE Rule 405—Know Your Client. If there is anybody that you don't feel good about, you have to let him go somewhere else. If it means that you lose some business, that's OK, because you will make it up somewhere else. That's the approach I take.

DORSEY: We are going into a business now where many firms feel the right path for a broker is to find assets and give them away to be managed by someone else. Most firms don't train their brokers to become adept at stock selection and management. I haven't seen many brokers who really didn't want to be good at what they do, but most just don't know how to go about it and eventually give up.

DEMENT: This may sound arrogant, but a smart and mature broker working with a smart and mature client can do better than most managed money products. Managed money costs money. There are expenses associated with it, and these guys have to look good quarter by quarter because the public, being fickle, will take their money and go somewhere else if performance is down. In my opinion, there is more turnover in portfolios and more expenses associated with managed money than there would be for the individual broker working with the good client, choosing the right stocks, and sticking with them. I think that I can, in general, outperform the managers. These are people who are getting a lot of money and are very smart people, and yet they're underperforming the averages.

DORSEY: I agree.

DEMENT: I have a lot of brokers and clients who tell me, hey, that's wonderful for the client, Jim, but this is a transaction-driven business, and if you're not doing any transactions you are going to starve. Well, that hasn't happened because when my clients make money and they know that I'm being honest with them, they're very happy to refer their friends and relatives to me. It has happened over and over again.

So I build the business that way, rather than transaction driven in the individual accounts. I don't mind buying a Coca-Cola or Johnson & Johnson for somebody and having him hold onto it for twenty years, because he gets rich doing it, and along the way he is sending his friends to me.

"There is a perception that stockbrokers sit around all day talking on two telephones, smoking cigars, and wearing expensive suits."

JIM DEMENT

DORSEY: Jim, do you utilize market timing? Do you do anything at all to mitigate risk in these accounts, or are you more inclined to buy more of the same stocks if the market corrects?

DEMENT: I am more inclined to buy good stocks when they are low. I am a heck of a lot smarter about all of this than I was twenty-five years ago, but I have never developed any faith in my ability or anyone else's to predict markets. I do know that good stocks continue to go up. A stock like Coca-Cola, for example, took the same hit in October of '87 that everything else did, down 20 percent in a day, but because the earnings trend was still strongly upward, the stock came right back and has gone to new highs since then. So I advise my clients to stick with it for life. They might take a few hits, but by and large they are going to come out ahead over a long period of time.

The public doesn't always buy the new car or the new house, but they will buy Gillette razor blades, Coca-Cola, and will probably go to McDonald's, even in hard times. If you can make 12 or 14 percent a year on average, and inflation is at 3 percent, you are going to end up making some money. If you do it patiently and don't try to force it, you end up doing just fine.

DORSEY: What kind of staff do you have in your ever-growing business? How do you manage that staff now?

DEMENT: I think that as a person grows his business, he reaches the point where he has enough clients, enough assets, and enough activity. He has to figure out ways to do it smarter without expanding work hours and staff, or if he is willing to build a team, hire more assistants, get more computers, all that sort of thing.

I like to keep it simple, and so I have an assistant, and I share that assistant with some other folks here at Davenport, but I have managed to keep my business of the size where I'm continuing to build it. I'm making a good living, I'm contributing to the profits of the firm, and I'm doing this as best I can in a normal work day, without having to take on a whole lot of extra staff and computers. And my own philosophy is I don't need all the money in the world. What I need is enough money to be comfortable, and then time to get to the gym, play with my grandchildren, read a book that has nothing to do with business, and in general experience my life beyond just the attempt to produce business. Other people have different approaches to it, but I like to keep it simple and to learn a little bit about what's going on in the world, stay healthy, and to spend time with the grandchildren, which is very important.

DORSEY: It certainly is.

DEMENT: Yes. So everybody makes that choice. And I have known some guys that built tremendous teams, and they are doing God-awful amounts of business, and all that. If that makes them happy, then fine, but that's not the path that I choose. I keep it very simple with just the one assistant.

I try to do a mailing every month or so after the statements have gone out. I will find some piece of financial information that I think is pertinent, and I will send it to all my clients and prospective clients with a little note that says, "I appreciate your business, and I would appreciate your referrals"—very low key, but it does work, because people won't think to refer others to you unless you ask.

DORSEY: Do you meet with all your clients once a quarter? With your approach, you probably don't need to.

DEMENT: Not necessarily. That's the beauty of having an understanding with your client. You both know that unless something goes terribly wrong, you're gong to hold onto a stock for years. For example, Nike is down. So I went back and looked at the fundamentals. Nike is still an A-rated company, with strong financials, and the thirty or forty analysts who follow the company say that the earnings are going to continue to grow at about 16 percent a year for at least the next five years. With financial strength and the earnings expectations like that, I am willing to take that temporary hit and not get scared out of the stock.

> *". . . Building a business doesn't come easily for most of us—we have to earn it."*
>
> JIM DeMENT

I've heard it said by Guy Williams, who used to run the finances for Signet Bank, that the best performing portfolios he ever experienced are those in which a little old lady inherits a bunch of blue-chip stocks from her husband, and she puts them in a lock-box and forgets about them for thirty years. I think there is an element of truth to that.

DORSEY: If you could give some advice to a new broker starting out, what would it be?

DEMENT: I would tell them not to expect the business to be easy. There is a perception that stockbrokers sit around all day talking on two telephones, smoking cigars, and wearing expensive suits. A new broker should have no illusions about sitting around raking in a lot of money. It's more of being an analyst than anything else. There is a lot of sales and marketing involved if you are going to be successful. And there's a lot of relationship building.

You have to be willing and able to serve people, and you have to want to help them. You also have to be ready for a lot of rejection and be ready to work very hard to constantly meet new people. After fifteen or twenty years, you'll build to the point where you may be making more money than you really deserve, but you will be making up for the early years when you were making a lot less than you deserved. Building a business doesn't come easily for most of us—we have to earn it.

DORSEY: You mentioned once that you talk to your daughters about how to live life in the best way possible, and I think it's something that a broker could apply to this business.

DEMENT: I talk to my girls about the principles by which we should live our lives, and what I usually tell them is that what works for me is the one that I embrace when I am a little unsure about things:

I fast forward in my mind to my deathbed scene, and I have about an hour to go. When I'm thinking back on my life I ask myself, "What did I do right, and what do I regret? Who do I want surrounding my bed right now? And finally, when I am gone, what do I want on my tombstone?" After having thought about these things for a few seconds, I then move myself back to the present time, and I find that it helps me to make sound decisions. It keeps things in perspective.

DORSEY: Well, you know, I think brokers could look at their businesses in a similar way. They should think about how they want to be remembered when they retire. When they look back, what will they want people to say about their abilities and what they did with their clients' accounts? Brokers should be cognizant of how they are perceived.

DEMENT: I think all of life is perspective, and I don't think we should allow ourselves to be forced in any direction that's going to be harmful to our health or family. We should be enjoying life beyond the acquisition of money. We all need some money, and we all want to help others make some money, but there is a balance to be achieved, and that's where it takes a little thoughtfulness from time to time.

DORSEY: Well, Jim, I can tell that you've got a lot more years left in this business. Thank you very much.

DEMENT: My pleasure.

JIM DeMENT is Vice President of Investments at Davenport & Co. in Richmond, Virginia. Prior to joining Davenport, he was a Vice President at Merrill Lynch in Richmond, where he was employed for nineteen years. Jim graduated from the U.S. Military Academy at West Point, then went on to earn three master's degrees from the University of Richmond and Western New England College. A highly decorated pilot, his service in the U.S. Air Force included 160 missions during the Vietnam War.

CHAPTER 4

BRINGING VALUE TO THE TABLE

WHEN I WAS A YOUNG BROKER in the 1970s, much of the value I brought to my customers came from the prestige of my firm. When I opened with a prospecting dialogue, I used the whole name of Merrill Lynch, Pierce, Fenner & Smith; it sounded powerful—it was powerful. Merrill was the biggest, and in most eyes the best, brokerage-house on Wall Street. The word on the street was that the large wirehouses would absorb the smaller ones with the big three eventually doing all the brokerage business. We knew that Merrill Lynch would be one of the three players.

But times have changed and, as usual, when a prediction becomes conventional wisdom it rarely happens. Instead of imploding, the brokerage business exploded. Today virtually all financial firms, insurance companies, CPAs, and even financial planners (qualified and nonqualified) are competing for the same customers. One of the most interesting results of the explosion is that brokers are going out on their own and clearing their business through a broker-dealer. Every major firm is providing the same services and the commissions that full service brokers charge are getting squeezed by discounters. The clout that a big firm business card added to the equation a few years ago is much less important today than the value that an individual broker brings.

> *"If the sum of what you bring to the table is the size of your firm and its intricate offerings—and all firms offer the same things—where is the value added for the customer?"*

THOMAS DORSEY

Investors who do their own research can easily trade on the Internet for $14 or less per trade. Fourteen dollars goes a long way, even with slippage of an eighth or quarter here and there. Just about all the information and analysis an investor needs is free on the Internet. Heck, for the cost of a one-year subscription to *Bloomberg Personal Finance* magazine—which I think is one of the best out there—our customer can get a mini-Bloomberg® system with filters, quotes, portfolio capabilities, and much more.

When an investor asks you what benefit he will derive from doing business with you rather than with some other broker, your response might be that XYZ Brokerage, where you work, is one of the largest on Wall Street. That was my response fifteen years ago. You have more institutional all-star research analysts than any other firm on the street. Perhaps you also have some wonderful computerized financial plans that can be tailored to your customers' needs, all for $150 per plan. Your commissions are very competitive, and you even provide checking and money market accounts. All financial transactions can be kept at one place. You can even provide a monthly statement of your customer's account with all financial transactions included on that statement.

His response to all this may be: "That sounds good, but the guy down the street at ABC Brokerage just told me the exact same thing, as did the guy at PDQ Brokerage." If the sum of what you bring to the table is the size of your firm and its intricate offerings—and all firms offer the same things—where is the value added for the customer? You'll need much more to compete in this competitive business climate. Your skills are what set you apart, not the prestige of your firm.

If you think your firm is unique, look around. I have seen tiny firms offer just about everything a large firm can, and more in some cases, for less money. Where's your edge?

I was speaking at the Major Firms Continuing Education Series recently. During lunch with a number of brokers I asked one gentleman what he did for his business. I was interested in what he thought defined his niche. He responded by telling me he was an asset gatherer. He raised money for other money managers through their in-house program. He said he was primarily a manager's manager. His clients paid him a fee to watch over the managers. This was his only input in the equation.

I felt a cold chill when I realized: He's spending his career riding on the bus looking out the window at others who are actively participating in the investment process. What if the managers with whom he placed money continued to do a good job? What is he managing? Why would a client continue to pay a percent or more for someone who was not adding any value? How long would it take before his firm began to cut his payout? When the business cycle turns down and his client is losing money, will he continue to feel the management fee is justified?

This broker has virtually no control over his business. I saw him as a line item that could be canceled out at any moment. I wouldn't sleep at night if I only provided a watch-dog service for my clients. His clients might soon find out that in order to outperform 75 percent of all money managers, they need only to buy the S&P Depository Receipts on the American Stock Exchange through a discount broker.

In Chapter 5, "Establishing Your Niche," Sam Lee of Salomon Smith Barney also raises assets for outside managers but keeps control of those assets. He is the determing factor as to whether the funds should rest in a money market fund within the program or be actively managed. His clients look to him to manage the market risk. Sam looks to the manager to make the stock selections. When the market risk is high, as it was in May 1998, Sam has the ability to move part or all of the funds to the money fund. This twist on the asset-gathering concept is what keeps Sam in control and provides added value. We'll expand on this concept in Chapter 5.

You will excel in this business by selling yourself. *You* are the product; you are the brand name. The added value that I am talking about runs much deeper than having a knowledge of your firm's products and services. In order to flourish in the 21st century, you will have to become a true craftsman at the investment process—someone who thoroughly understands the market and can successfully navigate the ups and downs. The long and short of it is, you will have to be able to make money for your clients—even in years when the market does not go up 30 percent.

Since 1987, over three trillion dollars in profits have been made in the equity markets. That's *equity* markets—not tax shelters, or kitchen sink bonds, insurance deals, or guaranteed no-lose treasuries. During the next fifty years I predict that the same trend will continue. Equities are where millionaires are made. Package products are where large fortunes are made into small fortunes. Every big producer I have ever met who consistently makes money for his clients has become a big producer by being well versed in the equity markets. I have seen some very large tax shelter producers in my time, but most aren't in the business today.

I believe that a broker can do just as well, if not better, than the majority of money managers. A broker simply has to add value. He must have the desire to be an active participant in the investment process and develop a logical, organized, easily understandable way of managing his clients' assets. It doesn't require a degree from MIT, either. There is so much information available today that one can become an expert in any area of investing, from financial planning to trusts and annuities. Whatever direction you choose, become an expert in it. Be the person others come to for advice on that subject.

"If you as a broker have nothing to offer

that is above and beyond your

competition, then you are on your

way out the door."

THOMAS DORSEY

There are two approaches to researching equities—fundamental analysis and technical analysis. To bring true value to the table for an equity investor, a broker must understand both of these schools of thought. Most brokers are familiar with the fundamental side of the equation, but know almost nothing of the technical side. Even the Series 7 examination is full of questions on fundamental analysis but has relatively little on technical analysis. Let's look for a moment at the technical side.

What causes the price of produce to change in the supermarket? Think about it for a second before you answer. Why are tomatoes more expensive in January than they are in July? The answer is that the growing season for tomatoes in most locales is the summer. In

January, tomatoes must be shipped in from warmer locales, which results in higher unit costs. The demand remains relatively constant, but the supply diminishes considerably, resulting in an increase in the prices you see at the store.

In the stock market, the supply remains relatively constant, but the demand fluctuates. An unchanged supply coupled with increased demand results in higher prices. If there are more buyers than sellers willing to sell, price rises. A specialist's job on the NYSE is to maintain an orderly market. If demand for his stock increases above the amount he can match with the sell orders that he has on the books, then he must step in and sell stock to accommodate the increased demand. How long do you think he will sell stock from his inventory at a constant price if demand continues to outpace supply? Not for long. He's not in the business of going out of business. He will raise the price of the stock until he can attract enough supply to accommodate the increased demand. The stock price will seek a higher level of equilibrium.

> *"The common threads you will find in each of the interviews in this book are the love of the business, a solid game plan, and the willingness to work hard."*
>
> THOMAS DORSEY

Here is where technical analysis comes in to play. Technical analysis endeavors to record, in various ways, the imbalance between supply and demand. Bar charts create certain patterns the same way Gann Angles, Elliott Waves, and Point and Figure charts do. Since we at Dorsey, Wright specialize in the Point and Figure charts, I can discuss only its concepts with authority. It is my passion for and mastery of Point and Figure that is a big part of the value that I personally bring to our clients.

The ways in which you differ from the broker down the street will define your business in the years to come. If you as a broker have nothing to offer that is above and beyond your competition, then you are on your way out the door. It won't take a CPA long to convince your customers that they are paying you far too much to act as a middle man. And guess what? Your friendly CPA is probably getting registered as an investment adviser as you read this. To stay in the game you need to figure out what value you can personally bring to your customers. Communicate that to your prospects and apply it to your clients. Most brokers I meet today can't begin to set themselves apart from the pack—but they'll need to learn how to do that in order to survive in the coming years.

INTERVIEW

Chris Guttilla, Lehman Brothers
New York, New York

I WOULD LIKE TO INTRODUCE one of the best stock-picking brokers in this business: Chris Guttilla is a broker with Lehman in New York City. When I think about Chris, I think of someone who is on fire about his business. He digs deeply into the stocks he recommends to his customers and knows virtually everything about them. He doesn't make a move unless the technical picture supports his fundamental work. The stocks he is involved in are fundamentally and technically sound. One of the most interesting things he adds is a unique perspective on insider buying. Chris also has a solid sell discipline. He is not afraid to be wrong and when he is, he takes immediate action.

The common threads you will find in each of the interviews in this book are the love of the business, a solid game plan, and the willingness to work hard. Chris has all of these positive attributes in spades. Let's get into his story.

TOM DORSEY: Chris, I've known you for years, and whenever I think of brokers I would give my account to, your name always comes to mind. Your story needs to be told. Let's just start at ground zero. How did you get started as a broker and how did you develop a strategy?

CHRIS GUTTILLA: When I started out in 1985, it was like throwing darts. I listened to whatever the firm liked as the hot stock of the day. I would call my clients and sell them the recommended stock. But it didn't take me long to realize that this strategy wasn't working. I needed something more, so I began to educate myself.

DORSEY: I know that you routinely apply technical analysis to your fundamental picks.

GUTTILLA: Yes, I can hear the greatest fundamental story in the world, but if it is not backed up by a Point and Figure buy signal in a column of Xs, I don't care, I'll wait.

In my experience at larger firms, using fundamental research without technicals behind it has led to some real disasters. For example, I was buying Union Carbide at the top of the sector move and at the top of UK's chart. That stock didn't see that high again for eight years. And had I known what I know today, I would never have made that mistake.

DORSEY: Tell me how you formulated an investment strategy.

GUTTILLA: I noticed that the biggest winners that Oppenheimer ever put out all had one thing in common: corporate insiders were aggressive buyers of the stock. For example, they had a great call on Bank of America, which was trading between $8 and $10 a share. They brought in a big heavyweight management team. Mr. Clousen was the chairman of the company. Everybody on Wall Street figured they were going out of business, and I watched this guy buy 10 million shares of stock over the course of six months—and I think the stock went from 10 to 300 in the next three years. So that was the first case that suggested I might change my fundamental approach. Buying the hot stock of the week wasn't getting me anywhere close to where I needed to be.

Each Monday morning the firm put out five stocks to buy. I don't know how they picked them, and I don't know what their methodology was, but we were just the salesmen. Because I was a young guy in the business, I didn't really know what else to do. I thought these guys were the gurus, and they knew it all. I had seen the analysts on TV, and I figured they were smarter than I was, so I'd better buy those stocks for my customers. I had no method, no game plan at all. After I finally developed a game plan, my business exploded. The plan was to concentrate on buying whichever stocks the insiders were buying. I'd take that list and match up the fundamentals with the technicals.

Now I can monitor twenty different stocks. I think insiders are the best judges of value in the stocks they are buying; however, their timing might not be good. I use technical analysis and, in particular, Point and Figure charts to help me decide when to buy and when to sell. It's worked quite successfully for us.

"If you don't believe in the company, how can you sell its stock to someone else?"

CHRIS GUTTILLA

DORSEY: Let's talk about how you built your business. How do you build relationships with your customers?

GUTTILLA: I go out and meet each person face-to-face.

DORSEY: You've built quite a positive reputation. I would guess that you have a very good referral business.

GUTTILLA: Yes, to a certain extent. I have evolved to a point where I have a profitable track record. I've been making money for my clients, so now my referral business is really starting to kick in and is now outpacing my telemarketing business. I need more support to help me service my customers now. So, in other words, half of my accounts are from telemarketing and half are from referral. I try to average ten accounts a month in new business.

DORSEY: How important is the personal connection between you and your clients?

GUTTILLA: A client gives me a chance to manage his money, and we see if we can build a relationship together. I'm trying to build a business relationship with people with whom I can see eye-to-eye. I have to trust him as much as he has to trust me. It's definitely a two-way street. When an account is committing to do business with me, I go out and see the person face-to-face.

DORSEY: How else do you prospect?

GUTTILLA: One method of prospecting is to network in your book by getting referrals from satisfied clients. Another way to prospect is to call people and present ideas that are associated with their industry. When Lucent Technologies was split off from AT&T, I called prospects in the telecommunications industry. I called executives from MCI to let them know that they could finally do business with Lucent Technologies because Lucent had gone public.

We called executives in all the major telecommunications companies and sent them the Lucent Technology prospectus. I didn't get any stock on the offering. It was a one-issue stock, so anybody could have bought it. And we opened up quite a few accounts simply by calling people who were in the industry that could now do business with Lucent Technology.

Possibly call the Chamber of Commerce for a list of names of executives in the area to call. I might call a prospect with an idea on the biggest company in Richmond, Virginia. The biggest company in Virginia is Philip Morris, so I often call people in Richmond to tell them that Phillip Morris stock is cheap. Michael Price just bought 5 percent of the company. When a great investor like Michael Price makes an investment in a company and I see that they have filed a 13 d, I'll call the company and try to find out what's behind the 13 d. For example, what does George Soros see in Waste Management that's attractive to him when everybody on Wall Street doesn't like it? I gain insight by looking into these questions.

DORSEY: When you prospect new clients, do you discuss technical analysis? Does that give you an edge or does it confuse them?

GUTTILLA: It definitely gives me an edge, because if I recommend AT&T or Waste Management, I can fax them a chart and it speaks for itself. They can easily see where the stock has been and get an idea of where it might go. Then all I have to do is give them the details of that particular situation. They can see that the stock peaked at $60, look over at the left-hand side of the stock, and see that it's bottomed down in this area between $30 and $35 a share six years in a row. This stock has never gone below 30. So they can see that this is the high and there is the low—you don't have to explain it.

You can make a recommendation to buy the stock with a stop point 15 percent or 20 percent below where it's trading, depending on their risk tolerance.

DORSEY: That's a lot of research that you do on your part. The value you bring to the table is substantial. That's what I mean when I talk about "value added."

GUTTILLA: I'm the guy who is ultimately under the gun. Even if the firm recommended a stock, the client is going to take his account elsewhere if I consistently lose money for him. I can tell him the analyst made the mistake, but my client doesn't care about that. I was the one who recommended it to him. Even though the firm is backing me up with the research, I'm the one who is going to lose the account, so I'm not going to trust somebody else to make that decision for me. If I'm going to be accountable, then I'm going to be the guy who does the research.

DORSEY: What types of events would cause you to reconsider a stock?

GUTTILLA: I look for a bunch of different things, but once I have initiated a trade and the stock goes up, I just follow the sector bullish percent all the way up as long as it remains positive. I'll typically hold the stock until it breaks its bullish support line. So I don't get out at the top, but I have found out that I can ride out market swings by allowing the trend line to be my sell action point. So, my first sell signal is when it breaks the bullish support line.

DORSEY: Let's say the sector bullish percent index rises above the critical 70 percent level and then reverses down into what we would call "defense." Do you continue holding the stock?

GUTTILLA: Oh, no. Then I batten down the hatches. I sell calls.

DORSEY: So in other words, you begin to manage the trade. When a sector's bullish percent index rises above 70 percent and reverses, it typically suggests all stocks underlying the sector are now suspect. It doesn't mean, however, that they have to go down. Selling calls would be one of my preferred defensive moves in such a situation.

GUTTILLA: When the sector gets to a level that suggests high risk, then I begin to use derivatives to possibly mitigate the risk or make the position more profitable. Each situation is different. I might also consider selling part of the position.

DORSEY: You prefer to *act* rather than *react*.

GUTTILLA: We got some great buys last year following the technology crash in the summer when the OTC stocks declined the equivalent of 1,000 Dow points in a matter of a couple of weeks. Software, semi's, computers, and lots of other groups were down below the critical 30 percent bullish level.

DORSEY: When you say, "down below the 30 percent bullish level," you are referring to the sector bullish percent indexes we use to guide our sector selection.

GUTTILLA: Exactly. When a sector gives you that kind of opportunity, having dropped to such a low level of stocks with buy signals, one simply has to buy the highest quality stock in the sector and let it go—stocks like Microsoft for software and Intel for semiconductors. That's how you attract investors to our style of investing. It's a simple sale. The sector is washed out as are the stocks underlying the sector. In conditions like this it's easy to open accounts on the phone. Microsoft is down 25 percent from its high, and it's the best stock in the sector. Windows 95 was actually when I began buying Microsoft. I thought that after they had $10 billion in sales, and Windows was supposed to be the next big product, I would buy the stock on the next good pullback. I don't chase stocks.

At that point I'll just call all the people in my book and let them know I'm buying Microsoft. My registered assistants will also call clients and tell them the same thing. We'll then work up a fundamental analysis of what is taking place with the company and get that out to the customers.

DORSEY: In 1996 there were a number of washed-out groups in that sell-off in the summer.

GUTTILLA: I simply bought the best companies in the groups that were near or below 30 percent.

DORSEY: And just sat back and let it happen?

GUTTILLA: Take 1992 for example, when the drug stocks were below 30 percent for the first time in a number of years.

DORSEY: I remember that we were pounding the table to buy them because they were below 30 percent bullish on the sector.

GUTTILLA: Right, and everybody said that with Clinton in as President the drug companies weren't going to be able to raise prices. Every analyst on Wall Street was so negative—all you had to do was look at the drug bullish percent at 30 percent and know you had to buy them. If you understand the concept of supply and demand, you realize that all these negative articles are being written right at the bottom. Just like the bank stocks in 1990—totally washed out, and Wall Street was saying there was no hope. Everybody thought they were going out of business and the Federal Reserve stepped in and lowered rates so the banks could re-liquefy. That was the fix. They can't let Citicorp go out of business.

DORSEY: You are talking about supply and demand imbalances. When a sector gets to a point at which there are less than 30 percent of the stocks underlying the sector on Point and Figure buy signals, everyone has sold who wants to sell. The availability of supply at that point to force the sector lower is extremely low. The problem is most investors buy high and hope to sell higher; the whole idea is to buy low and sell high. That's exactly what you are trying to do: Focus on sectors that are low and then simply buy the best stocks in those sectors.

GUTTILLA: That's what happened at AT&T when they fired the chief operating officer they had hired just a few months earlier. If you were watching AT&T trade, the stock was $35. It didn't go down after that news. That was the lowest the stock had traded in thirty days. It's up to $44. The stock was in the green zone—washed out, at the bottom. The chart tells it all. I had been recommending the stock and it's one of the Dogs of the Dow, which is a strategy of buying the five lowest-priced, highest-yielding stocks in the Dow Jones and then holding them for a year. The strategy had averaged 20 percent for the last twenty-five years.

After all the bad news was out, I was watching the stock trade, and the stock was in a historic area where it's bottomed before. I called my customers and said, "The news is not going to get any worse for AT&T than it is today. Buy the stock." Lo and behold, it's up eight points in thirty days.

DORSEY: AT&T has learned to fail fast, and that's important in today's business environment. That's a great story. Thinking like that is what I mean by bringing value to the table. That's how a broker differentiates himself from the rest of the pack, having a logical, organized method of investing—rather than simply parroting what research is saying. The idea is to work as a team. Research does the fundamental work, you overlay your own fundamental work and then allow the roadmap—technical analysis—to guide the trade. To survive in this business in the years ahead, a broker will have to become a craftsman—like the customers' men in the early 1990s.

GUTTILLA: Right. So when you go out and meet the customer and you have had a few successful trades, it becomes much easier to develop a relationship. When you have a plan of attack you can call people with confidence. People feel comfortable when they have a good broker and they are dealing in blue-chip names.

> *"So there are just a million ways to get leads. You just have to be creative. If you are buying Lucent Technology, call other officers in the telecommunications industry. People like to buy what they know."*
>
> CHRIS GUTTILLA

DORSEY: What kind of staff do you have, and how do you manage them?

GUTTILLA: We have a full-time sales assistant who is registered, and she has been with me for ten years now. She handles all the back office problems—money, dividends, and those kind of details. If a client needs something, they will usually call her directly. If it's not related to the market, my sales assistant handles it. So I try to separate the back office business from the market analysis. I oversee it every day, but I don't get involved in the details.

DORSEY: Let's discuss how you view the overall market, in particular, the New York Stock Exchange bullish percent. The higher it gets, the less aggressive you become, and you become more aggressive when it is low.

GUTTILLA: You'll never be able to pick the top or the exact bottom, but we get close. But if you can work in that 80 percent curve that we always talk about, this is when you have to start buying. If you don't believe in the company, how can you sell its stock to someone else? When the risk level is high in the market, it is better to spend your time developing leads than to open new accounts and place them in harm's way right off the bat.

DORSEY: Do you use your firm's fundamentals, *Value Line's*, Standard & Poor's, or any mix of services?

GUTTILLA: I use everything possible. Fortunately, Lehman has its own research department with about thirty-five analysts. They don't like to cover big blue-chip stocks. They don't think they have an edge on it, so they will cover some secondary or tertiary stocks in the industry, and their research is good. To supplement that we buy research from big name broker-dealers.

On top of that, you can get the JAG Notes (www.jagnotes.com) every day, and you can see exactly what people are buying and selling. And there are services like the Bloomberg® system that have any Wall Street report you want. So the information is out there.

DORSEY: We've discussed how you manage trades. What about some of the timeless strategies like the Spiders or the Dogs of the Dow? How do these types of strategies find their way into any of your business?

GUTTILLA: I have started to put smaller investors into the Dogs of the Dow, just because the strategy has worked so well and it's a more diversified way to invest. In the past, I've told smaller accounts and prospects to buy Michael Price's mutual fund, because he is one of the smartest guys in the world. He makes money, but he is not trying to outperform the market. He makes between 15 and 18 percent year after year, whether it's a good market or a bad market [Price has recently retired]. But now I've started to sell the Dogs of the Dow, which I think is perfect for somebody who wants to invest $25,000 or for somebody who wants to invest for college planning, trust accounts.

We look at it as a kind of anchor. It simply keeps you in quality stocks that will take the fear factor out of the mix. You must hold the portfolio for one year.

DORSEY: What would you say is your biggest competition?

GUTTILLA: I think my biggest competition right now would be discounters. I have a feeling that some of my accounts might trade away from me at discount houses. Sometimes an account will ask me about a stock recommended to them long ago and I've already been stopped out of it. The stock is much lower now and they want advice on what to do with it. They must have bought some away from me and were not advised to sell it when something went wrong. So some of my good customers trade away at discount houses and that's a problem. They probably trade at E-Trade on the Internet. I need to pay attention to bringing in all of their assets.

DORSEY: Interesting. Chris, tell me what a typical day for you would be like.

GUTTILLA: It's pretty regimented. On the 6:10 A.M. train, I read *The Wall Street Journal* and *The New York Times*. When I arrive at Lehman I print out *The Daily Equity-Market Analysis Report*, by Dorsey, Wright. I take a look at all the trades from the previous day to make sure they were confirmed and there are no mistakes. I work out for an hour, so by the time I come back to the office at 8:30, I've already read all the pages of your report. I've set up my business plan for the day, and I start by 8:30.

DORSEY: Why do you say you have to work out?

GUTTILLA: It keeps me energized. I think you have to be in good shape. It's a high-energy business, and it takes a lot of energy to run your business. You have to go out there and deal with so many people each day.

For instance, this morning I had news out on a few stocks, I literally had eight lines holding. It takes a lot of energy to talk to eight different investors about news out on a stock they have an interest in. I know that if I am to have a good day I have to work out. It's a high-stress business. I have to make sure I eat right and exercise right so I can be productive.

DORSEY: Okay, now it's 8.30 A.M.?

GUTTILLA: It's 8:30, I'm back in the office. I make a list of ten clients I haven't called in a while with the intention of calling them that day with an idea I'm working on. And I'll make sure before I go home that I call all those investors. A lot of brokers use Broker's Ally. It's a software program available that makes it easy to keep track of all your clients. It helps you know when the last time was that you spoke to this or that client or sent him something. Basically it keeps track of all contact you make with a client. It helps a broker stay more organized. But I'm really not that automated yet. I'm getting more automated as the days go by. I use the old way, you know, manually look through your positions and accounts. I do keep track of my inventory but I still look it up manually.

So the most important thing for me is to be sure I contact the ten people every day. I call them with ideas or discussions of where the market is. I make sure my team is working, and they know exactly what they are doing. I make sure my interns search out a certain number of leads each day. I call it the "Rule of Sixes." Every day my guys have to make six presentations, and they have to get six new leads or else they have to work on Saturday. Because if you do the numbers as I was taught in the beginning, you will succeed. If you get six leads every day, five days a week, that's thirty leads. There are four weeks in a month. That's 120 leads. If you make six pitches a day, you are making 120 presentations each month. Now, if you have a good lead, you should be able to close if you are a good salesman. You know, I'm not a great salesman, but I used to close 50 percent of the leads that I pitched. So this guy could be the worst salesman and close 10 percent and still open twelve new accounts a month.

"It's been a great market for trading. With more and more high-tech stocks coming on the scene, I expect the environment to be ripe for this type of activity for quite some time."

THOMAS DORSEY

DORSEY: Who makes up your staff, Chris?

GUTTILLA: Joanne takes care of all the administration. I have John, who is my senior trainee, and I have a new trainee. The new trainee does all the legwork. If I wanted to prospect in Richmond, Virginia, he would call the Chamber of Commerce in Richmond and begin to develop leads. He might look for sales volume in companies of more than $5 million. We would then contact the owner of the company, or the president, to determine if he would like to hear from us from time to time. And if we are calling Richmond, Virginia, we would recommend Philip Morris if the stock fit all our parameters for purchase. We would try to develop a relationship that way. So he does all the legwork. We call investors involved in Rule 144 stocks. These 144s are filed every day. We are more interested in filings from thirteen months ago, or sixteen months. Officers don't move around too much. So if an officer is selling stock in a company we'll call him up. We also order *Vickers Stock Research* where one can order the 144 sales for a whole year. So there are just a million ways to get leads. You just have to be creative. If you are buying Lucent Technology, call other officers in the telecommunications industry. People like to buy what they know.

DORSEY: So when they get this lead, is the lead called that day?

GUTTILLA: Well, there are two different leads. We are talking about building up a lead source.

DORSEY: OK.

GUTTILLA: So, we can go qualify the lead. If he is qualified, we will call him. One trainee is always building up the lead source and another trainee is calling that lead source.

DORSEY: So, they turn from suspect to prospect?

GUTTILLA: Exactly.

DORSEY: So, let's go back to your typical day, then. So they are getting leads throughout the day, you are having talks with at least ten people that you haven't talked to before or at least for a good while?

GUTTILLA: Right.

DORSEY: Your own customers?

GUTTILLA: Yes.

DORSEY: You are making stock recommendations and managing existing positions.

GUTTILLA: Exactly. I have accounts that I consider long-term type investors, and I have more aggressive traders. My book value falls into one of those categories where 80 percent of my revenues are generated by 20 percent of my book, and I'm always trying to get other clients into that 80 percent bracket.

DORSEY: That percentage is pretty universal in the industry.

GUTTILLA: So, there are certain investors who are long-term, buy-hold, never-want-to-sell type accounts, which is fine. So when AT&T is down and out, you buy them AT&T. So I have to constantly keep those investors in mind, and then I have to manage the active traders that will trade away from you if you don't have ideas.

DORSEY: So you deal with active traders also?

GUTTILLA: Yes.

DORSEY: You have your longer-term investors who will buy the American Telephone & Telegraph and Waste Management, but you have got the traders who are looking to you for trading ideas?

GUTTILLA: Right.

DORSEY: What's hot and what's not today?

GUTTILLA: Exactly.

DORSEY: What would you say the percentage of your business is from trading?

GUTTILLA: 70 percent. I am a very active broker.

DORSEY: That's interesting. It's been a great market for trading. With more and more high-tech stocks coming on the scene, I expect the environment to be ripe for this type of activity for quite some time.

GUTTILLA: Yes. So that's why we work from an inventory of stocks like any other business. You always have to be reading, searching for new good ideas. The breakout page in your report helps quite a bit in this endeavor. If you see a stock break out and you know the fundamentals behind the story, you can get on the phone immediately.

DORSEY: Have you used the searches on our Internet charting system yet?

GUTTILLA: I haven't really been automated on the Internet, no. I do it all manually. So my day is constantly changing. For example, the AT&T trade that we just spoke about, that was a two-day time where I just got on the phone and I had a list of 100 investors we needed to speak to. My registered trainees were on the phone calling my long-term clients explaining why we were buying AT&T, and I was on the phone calling my trading clients. We bought a lot of that stock. When you have an opportunity like that we can buy 100,000 shares in two days. So you have to be able to mobilize very quickly.

> ## *"You control your own destiny in this business. It's unlimited upside."*
>
> CHRIS GUTTILLA

DORSEY: Where do you think this business is going for the broker? What do you see in the future?

GUTTILLA: You control your own destiny in this business. It's unlimited upside. Did you know George Soros started out as a stockbroker? He made $800 million last year. That's the top paid man on Wall Street. If you want to be George Soros, you can be George Soros. So it's totally open-ended. That's what's so exciting about the business. The harder you work, the more you learn, and the better you are going to do for your clients. So, I continue to think that the business is going to be volatile, but if you have a game plan, it's the greatest business in the world.

DORSEY: In other words, this is not the kind of business where a lot of people get registered and sit down waiting for the phone to ring? This is hard work?

GUTTILLA: This is a 24-hour-day job, seven days a week, and it's exciting, and it changes every day. So there is always something different, there is always something to look at. Every day there is something new that happens on Wall Street. It's the greatest business in the world. You are an entrepreneur in your own business. You might work at Merrill Lynch, but they are your customers, you are the business owner. Merrill Lynch doesn't make you money. Merrill Lynch doesn't make you get on the phone. They will fire you if you don't get on the phone, but you control your own destiny, and that's the kind of business that we are in right now.

DORSEY: So you are the individual that makes it or breaks it yourself?

GUTTILLA: Absolutely.

A Vice President Private Client Services with Lehman Brothers, CHRIS GUTTILLA is located in New York City. He began his financial career in 1984 upon graduating from the University of Delaware with a degree in accounting. Chris's investment philosophies hinge largely on insider buyer analysis coupled with the Point & Figure methodology.

CHRIS GUTTILLA IS now employed by Lehman Brothers Inc. in its Private Client Services Group. The statements in the interview are those of Mr. Guttilla and do not necessarily reflect the views of his current employer.

Dennis H. Nelson, U.S. Bancorp Piper Jaffray
Topeka, Kansas

DENNIS NELSON, THE BRANCH MANAGER of U.S. Bancorp Piper Jaffray in Topeka, Kansas, is without a doubt one of the best branch managers and brokers I have met in the business. Dennis manages his branch as I would if I were a branch manager. I met Dennis at the Dorsey, Wright Stockbroker Institute that we hold three times a year here in Richmond, Virginia.

The value his group brings to the table is having a solid method of selecting what to buy and then having an in-depth understanding of supply and demand to help answer the all-important questions of when to buy and when to sell. He has a strategy that I think can be applied elsewhere in the business.

Dennis has created a method of evaluating stocks called "Val-Tech," which is a combination of fundamental value-oriented stocks with technical analysis overlaid for timing. The vast majority of brokers in his office used this selection process as their method of stock selection and management. If a customer walked into that branch and asked any of these brokers what to do with $200,000, he would likely get the same answer from each broker. This method of analysis has worked well for them, and the returns to their customers have been outstanding by any standard. Their selection process involves using only:

◆ *Value Line* rank 1 or 2 for timeliness
◆ growth rates of 20 percent or more
◆ returns on equity of 20 percent or more
◆ P/E ratios of less than 70 percent of the growth rate.

This is the inventory they work from. They then fit the Point and Figure method of market analysis, sector rotation, and individual stock charts to these value stocks. As the market rises, the inventory decreases in size as P/E ratios get out of range. As sectors decline or the market declines, more stocks show up on their value screen and the inventory inflates. It's almost self-managing. The size of their inventory is relatively small as their value screen is stringent. This keeps them from becoming mired down in trying to manage the 10,000 stocks trading on all exchanges.

This is one of the problems most brokers have: operating in a universe of thousands of stocks. Dennis has found a way to cut that monster down to a manageable size. Let's get to the interview with Dennis so he can explain in his own words how his system works.

> ## *"When I look back I find that the best accounts I have ever had were obtained from referral."*
>
> DENNIS NELSON

TOM DORSEY: Dennis, you're a veteran in this business. Tell me how it all began for you.

DENNIS NELSON: Well, I started in the brokerage business February 8, 1965, when I went to work for a firm called Barrett, Fitch, North. They were an old, smaller firm based in Kansas City. They had three or four offices in Lawrence, Wichita, and surrounding areas. I was right out of college. A couple of years later, in 1966, we opened an office in my hometown, Topeka. One of the reasons they hired me was because they wanted to have a presence in Topeka. In 1967 PaineWebber bought out Barrett, Fitch, North, and then as time went on, I became an assistant manager in Topeka. In 1974 I was asked to go manage the office in Tulsa for PaineWebber.

DORSEY: How did you develop your retail business early on in your career? I want to talk about your early broker years before we get into branch managing.

NELSON: At a small firm like Barrett, Fitch, North there really wasn't much sales training. I remember having one hour-long meeting in the conference room with a couple of older brokers—and that was the extent of the sales training. You were sort of on your own.

I learned the business from a book, and I wish I could remember the name of it now, on how to sell securities. It was very basic stuff like calling leads, introducing yourself, asking them if they have any interest in the market. If the response was positive, you probed further. We tried to find out what kinds of things they might be interested in. We would send that information out, follow up, and hope to open an account at some point in the future. I had a call sheet, and when I left for Tulsa I had a stack of daily call sheets that I hated to leave behind, but I tossed them.

There was a lot of work involved. I would try to call at least thirty people each day and see two more face-to-face. A similar method is used today; I think the Broyles System and some other programs are similar. It's just basically getting on the phone and contacting as many people as possible. It's a numbers game.

I think the best way to develop business is through referrals, and they are a result of doing a good job for current customers. When I look back I find that the best accounts I have ever had were obtained from referral.

DORSEY: Did you aspire to become a branch manager at that point, or did it just kind of fall into your lap?

NELSON: My experience is that even at a fairly young age I was a leader, for whatever reason. I can remember instances in grade school and Cub Scouts and Boy Scouts, and so on, where I tended to lead the pack. Churches I belonged to, I ended up being president of congregations on occasion. I've always enjoyed being in a leadership role. And so when I was asked to get involved in the management process, it was something that I wanted to do. However, I think we all have to recognize that in this business, branch managers sometimes experience all the grief and none of the glory. There has been a tendency a lot of times to take pretty good producers who have solid relationships with clients, and take them out of production and move them to a different city. I really missed the market. Although I was there every day, there is nothing like dealing with the market. That's why I think management, in our business, from the very top down, should spend some time in the branch and actually prospect a week or two out of the year so they can keep a pulse on what it's like with the troops.

DORSEY: Good idea. Although I'm afraid it would fall on deaf ears.

NELSON: When I was still in Topeka in the late 1960s I started to take Chartcraft—which was Point and Figure charting.

DORSEY: Were you a manager at this point or still a broker?

NELSON: I was an assistant manager, basically a broker. I remember back then getting the little manual on how to Point and Figure chart. Point and Figure charts shout for action. So I started charting stocks back then on a Point and Figure basis and found it to be helpful. However, when I moved to Tulsa, all that kind of went out the window. I went to Tulsa toward the bottom of the bear market, and most of my time was spent recruiting and educating on PaineWebber procedures.

DORSEY: Tell me about '74 as a broker. It was a market that most brokers today have never seen.

NELSON: The market didn't go down suddenly like in October '87. 1987 was a bear market that ended in a few days. This bear market lasted more than a year. The indices were different then. They weren't in the thousands. We were below 1,000. It was basically 25 points a week, just constant, constant eroding, where almost nothing ever went up. There was no glimmer of hope, and you rarely had a portfolio that had anything that had appreciated.

We pretty much lived by doing secondary issues of utilities and going for equities that had income. In other words, we tried to appeal to the income side of investing rather than the growth side.

We would get little spurts of activity. Back then rest homes and computers would have little spurts of activity and rise, but it was fairly short term and then you were punished because the general market was in a downtrend. That's why I feel it is important to look at the general trend of the market before anything else. Is it going up or is it going down? Then you look at individual groups and determine which ones are near bottoms and lastly, you look at individual stocks.

DORSEY: It was a pretty extreme market.

NELSON: Back then we had to struggle to survive. Brokers in New York City and all across the country were taking second jobs. Up until that time the New York Stock Exchange prohibited having another vocation, but it started making exceptions. Stockbrokers were driving cabs. I don't remember numbers, but as I recall, the number of registered brokers in this country dropped in half during that period. It was just a lousy business.

DORSEY: What made you want to stay after that kind of start?

NELSON: Well, when the management opportunity came up in Tulsa, I took it because I wanted to do something in the business other than commissions work. The salary thing might have appealed to me, although the salary that I was given wasn't more than I was making as a commissioned stockbroker. I was thinking about my family and the security of a salary. Tulsa was supposed to be a pretty good office; however, they had had tough times like everyone else. They had five or six brokers and only one of them was making more than minimum wage. But over a period of three years I managed to hire some new people. I had the office running by 1977. However, I was still making the same dismal salary and my family needs were growing. I didn't see any future in staying as a branch manager for a major wirehouse at that time, so I quit and moved back to Topeka and went into banking.

I managed portfolios for four banks. Although I was buying government and municipal bonds for the banks' portfolios and running some trust business, I missed the action of the investment business. So I had an opportunity in 1979 to go to work for a small firm in Topeka that was started back in 1934, called Beecroft, Cole. It was a very small firm. It had an office only in Topeka, with two or three good brokers, and one I was especially fond of. He was a fellow by the name of A. B. Woody.

> *"Back then we had to struggle to survive.*
>
> *Brokers in New York City and all across*
>
> *the country were taking second jobs. "*
>
> DENNIS NELSON

DORSEY: Did he have an impact on how you do business?

NELSON: Yes. Woody was in his eighties and liked to do stock analysis. He would get out spreadsheets and develop various ways of identifying an industry group's best stocks, and then proceed to call people to inform them he was buying those stocks. I remember back in the early '80s, interest rates had gone sky high. Inflation, which had been a huge problem, was starting to level out, and there was some talk that it might come down a little bit. Mr. Woody determined that utility stocks might be a good place to be. So he would get out *Value Line* research, which is all that the firm could afford at that time. He would do these spreadsheets, and he would write down P/E ratios and all kinds of safety ratings and cash flow per share and all these fundamental readings. This work would narrow down the list. This process fascinated me immediately because he came up with some good ideas. He would start off with forty or fifty stocks, and he would filter through them. There was an article in *Barron's* magazine back in the early 1970s about a trust officer in Chillicothe, Missouri, who on almost an annual basis won the stock market contest that *Barron's* used to sponsor. The interview with the old boy was quite fascinating, because he didn't have all the bells and whistles of the sophisticated wirehouses and research firms and the financial centers of the country. He had *Value Line.* That's all he had. He said, "I take the 1s and 2s on *Value Line,* and then I narrow it down to the ones that are expected to grow 20 percent a year. And then I look at the P/E ratio as compared to the growth rate, and if the P/E ratio is less than 70 percent of the growth rate, then I put that on a list of ones to look at pretty hard."

> *"The thing about charting is you need to have a feel for or the knowledge of what certain technical formations mean, and you have to work with it. It takes an education."*
>
> DENNIS NELSON

In other words, if a company is growing 20 percent, he didn't want to buy a stock that was selling over fourteen times earnings. That's the 70 percent of the growth rate of the P/E. Then he said, "I would look at a chart, and if it looked like it was going up, I would buy it." This fellow was up something like 77 percent that year. I mean, he would just beat the pants off of everybody. Woody remembered the article, too, and so we started playing with *Value Line.* We went with the 20 percent growth, the P/E no more than 70 percent of the growth rate, and something that Woody felt was very important as well—the return on stockholder equity. He felt like that was something that was critical in stock analysis and buying value. We played with various numbers, but in order to get the list down to a reasonable number of items, we settled on a return on stockholders' equity of 20 percent as something we wanted the company to exhibit, as well as the other features.

That's pretty much how we still do it in the Topeka office at

Piper Jaffray. We go through the *Value Line* database weekly and search for stocks that meet those criteria. We started doing the process in 1984 and did very well. We didn't do much technical analysis. We would buy them if they were 1s and 2s, and when they became 3s we sold them. That was similar to what the trust officer in Chillicothe, Missouri, did. However, as you probably are thinking, we often would ride a good idea up and see it come all the way down and maybe end up with a loss when it would become a 3, and it was a shame. There had to be something else that we should be doing in order to achieve performance. In 1992 Piper acquired our firm in Topeka, and although they have research, we continued to use our process to come up with ideas on a weekly basis.

DORSEY: You weren't the branch manager when Piper Jaffray took over?

NELSON: Yes. I was the president of Beecroft, Cole, and then I became the branch manager for Piper Jaffray in Topeka.

DORSEY: And then that's where I met you.

NELSON: Right, I think it was '93–94. Your Point and Figure charting is what turned a light on with me, because that was the piece of the puzzle that was missing.

DORSEY: This method is something you had used before if I'm not mistaken.

NELSON: Yes, I had experienced it and knew it was helpful, and really hadn't revisited for a lot of years, but we started reading the daily work from your company which was coming via Piper. Your report caused us to think about charts again. The thing about charting is you need to have a feel for or the knowledge of what certain technical formations mean, and you have to work with it. It takes an education.

DORSEY: In other words, it's not an overnight procedure.

NELSON: It's not an overnight thing. You need to experience it. And as time went on, we began to realize that using the charts in connection with our fundamental work with *Value Line* was working well. Now we look for company data from several sources. However, *Value Line* still provides us with most of the ideas. When the Dorsey, Wright product came to Piper, we started easing into how we were going to use the information. And there was a sufficient number of people in the office who felt that it was something they wanted to learn more about. I started sending the brokers one by one to the Dorsey, Wright Stockbroker Institute. I went first, and then sent others. We basically have a fairly cohesive group that uses the fundamental methods we developed many years ago. The difference now is we also use technical analysis on a daily basis.

> *"Our inventory is like an accordion, expanding, then contracting. Sectors move in and out of season."*
>
> D E N N I S   N E L S O N

DORSEY: Well, that's what I noticed when I came to visit your branch office. One of the things that hit me right between the eyes was the cohesiveness of the group. When we went into the morning meeting the majority of the brokers came in with their own books of both fundamental and technical research. They all had their own charts that they maintain themselves, and everybody was basically reading from the same page. Was this where you coined the term "ValTech" for your methods?

NELSON: Yes, value. Stocks that had value, or *Value Line,* if you want to use it in that way. Mainly we were trying to find stocks that had fundamental value, and then tech with the technical analysis, so

"ValTech" is what we call our process. I should also mention that this process primarily uncovers stocks that today would be considered mid- or small-cap type names. And if you take 1997 when it was a big-cap market, we didn't perform as well as you might think we should. I mean, we did very well, but we are looking for companies that have a P/E that's not as high as the growth rate, and the blue-chip Nifty Fifty doesn't fall into that range.

DORSEY: So the Nifty Fifty doesn't fall into the value category you search for. There have been a handful of large-cap stocks that have outperformed of late. I think this is directly due to the problems Asia and Russia are experiencing. It's simply a stampede into anything that has a name anyone can recognize. This also presents opportunity in the smaller-cap issues that are being overlooked. At some point they will gain sponsorship.

NELSON: We have had some of the big names like IBM and Coca-Cola. I suppose on an adjusted basis—we bought Coca-Cola in 1989 below $5. It came up using our process. Pepsi-Cola has also fallen into the value category. When the markets get extremely high, our list is not as long as it is when the market as a whole is at lower levels. It's a self-correcting mechanism. When the market is high we have less to buy and thus less to risk and when the market is low we have a wide range of opportunities simply by the P/Es fluctuating in and out of our parameters for buy candidates. In some market conditions we take some time to become fully invested. Our inventory is like an accordion—expanding, then contracting. Sectors move in and out of season.

DORSEY: Tell me more about how you use fundamental analysis.

NELSON: We try to find out everything we can about the company. We don't necessarily write for annual reports and things like that, but we go through recent news stories, recent earnings reports. We look at Standard & Poor's to see if its estimates are similar to *Value Line*'s. We look at other research that our firm provides from Goldman Sachs, DLJ, and our firm's own research to see if they follow that company and read everything we can about that company. If everything looks okay, we will put it on the master list.

DORSEY: Then you integrate technicals?

NELSON: Yes. The list is further broken down into list 1, 2, and 3. And list 1 contains stocks where the fundamental and the technical analyses are in line, including stocks that have positive relative strength, or if the relevant strength has been on a sell, we look for it to start improving by shifting into a column of Xs. It can still make the list on that basis. We like to see the industry group in one of the bullish modes, and we get the chart updated and put it in front of us, I'll just look at it and see if it feels right. It's my call. The stocks on the number 1 list are the ones that we would buy today. Most weeks there are only three or four stocks having all of the factors coming together. If a new client came in the door today, we might have to tell him that it takes a few months to get fully invested. We don't push the envelope; we buy what is right at this time and nothing else. If an investor comes in with $100,000, we aren't going to buy two stocks and let it go at that. Our process dictates that we buy 5 percent of the person's investable cash per position, so we want to hold about twenty stocks. Sometimes it gets to be a few more than that or a few less, but we are trying to have a portfolio with twenty stocks in at least five or six different industries.

This process we've developed helps us manage risk and enhance return. Then you have your individual client needs, a taxable account versus a qualified plan that you're investing for like an IRA. If it's a taxable account, as long as that stock is above the bullish support line, we could ride it for years, regardless of how high it goes or how much it might correct down toward the bullish support line. With tax-sensitive accounts we tend to keep our positions intact. As long as it's in that basic direction, we are there for a while. If the client isn't tax sensitive, or if it is a qualified plan, we tend to follow the DWA procedure of averaging out: If the stock is up 30 percent, we will sell a third of the position off the table. After another 30 percent, we will sell another third and then ride the balance until something happens such as a technical sell and break of the trendline.

We become very watchful of these things. If a stock drops with *Value Line* or the growth rate doesn't seem to be there but the stock is still rising we will sell at the first sign of technical trouble. A lot of that comes from working with the system, and I think it doesn't take too long before you realize that if a stock just goes up, it gets way beyond your criteria. All of a sudden the P/E is selling at 200 percent of your growth rate; then you need to protect that profit. If there is a change in the relative strength to negative we will take some profits, even in the tax-sensitive accounts.

"The first line of defense is hiring the right brokers."

DENNIS NELSON

DORSEY: Let's say that fundamentally a stock no longer qualifies for our inventory, that the price-earnings ratio has gone up too high. It will come out of your inventory, but it doesn't necessarily come out of an individual's portfolio? You will manage that position as long as you can?

NELSON: Yes. The master list will still show those stocks that are no longer fundamentally buys, but they will go to list 3, which means they are technically still on the rise, but they no longer meet our fundamental criteria.

When the fundamental readings get way too high we have to protect the positions. That's often where our best gains are. There is also a case where we might have a stock on the master list and never buy it because the technical never came around to a buy signal. We have done well over the years, but there are always ways to enhance or improve, and you have always got to look for new ideas. It's been especially gratifying to me to help train new brokers. They get training at Piper in the home office initially but they really don't get into this type of training.

DORSEY: I don't think any firm does. But I really like this process— It's defined, logical, and organized. It's something that makes your services more valuable to customers. More reliable.

NELSON: Yes. There is nothing better than the feeling of knowing how the whole process works and how a particular stock recommendation was determined. At times, only the analyst knows why the stock is recommended. For a new broker without a system there's a terrible feeling of confusion and lack of control. Over time it makes the broker gun-shy. In my branch we get the newer brokers involved with this process as soon as possible after they return from their initial training in the home office. I think it's helpful to them to develop a clientele using a solid, logical, organized plan rather than to simply shoot from the hip. You can't build a long-lasting business without a sensible plan of attack.

DORSEY: One thing I wanted to talk about was broker training. I know you touched earlier on what your brokers do, but one of the most important parts of this business in the period ahead is going to be education for brokers.

NELSON: The first line of defense is hiring the right brokers. Times have changed a little bit in my thirty-some years in the business. Today brokers need to be able to type, to gather information on their desk as needed, and to keep daily notes on everything that is going on. Brokers must have good common sense to succeed. Brokers also need to be extremely honest and ethical. We don't want people whose sole goal is to make money for themselves, because the broker's primary objective is to make money for his clients, and in turn, he will service his own needs. The client must always come first, no matter what. Brokers today have to be well versed in other financial products such as insurance, investment planning, and the computerized models of asset allocation and financial needs analysis. And the broker needs to be able to sit down and explain those things in a fairly concise and efficient manner.

DORSEY: Has the proliferation of information on the Internet had any affect on your business? Commissions with the online firms are so low they are basically a commodity.

NELSON: I don't know. I haven't had anybody tell me that they were transferring their account to a discount broker or investing on the Internet. Maybe it's the nature of my clients. They rely on me to do the work. There is still an enormous number of people out there who want help. We could probably buy our car on the Internet, too, but we still want to talk to someone with knowledge.

DORSEY: You've been extremely successful in this business. What can you impart to younger brokers to help them achieve this level of success in the future?

NELSON: To be successful in this business you have got to be in it for awhile and develop a feel for it. You've got to develop an understanding of what your talents are, and then cater to those people who appreciate your specific talents.

DORSEY: Well, Dennis, I want to thank you very much for the interview. It's going to give brokers some great ideas on managing their equities and adding value to their business.

DENNIS NELSON has served investors for over thirty years. Currently branch manager of U.S. Bancorp Piper Jaffray's Topeka, Kansas, office, he urges his clients to focus on growth of capital and income rather than short-term gains. He holds a bachelor's degree in business administration from the University of Kansas and participates in many local civic clubs.

ESTABLISHING YOUR NICHE

SCOTT BOWERS DIDN'T start out at the top of his field. He had a number of disastrous experiences on his way to becoming an excellent broker. The words "will to succeed" aptly describe Scott Bowers. And in the process of building his business he has developed a powerful niche.

Scott's methods are a little different from those of the mainstream broker. He works closely with CPAs. His outsourcing ideas might just work for you. It's a wide-open field in which the client, CPA, and broker all win. In today's investment environment, it is difficult to be an expert in all fields. Outsourcing makes a lot of sense, because each party brings a particular expertise to the table without having to give up control of clients or assets. Scott has learned to thrive in this new environment. What really caught my eye was his dedication to excellence and commitment to his clients. I don't think any of Scott's clients mind paying full commission for his services. I hope you find a way to incorporate some of his ideas into your business.

INTERVIEW

R. Scott Bowers, PaineWebber, Inc.
Houston, Texas

TOM DORSEY: Scott, how did you first get into the business?

SCOTT BOWERS: It was actually the inspiration of desperation. I had several false starts at becoming a syndicator of private placements and I was ready for a more stable line of work. I had just finished an MBA, and I wanted to get my CPA designation, so I went to work for Price Waterhouse in New York.

After four years of public accounting, I decided to specialize in real estate, and I wanted to syndicate properties using private placements to raise money. I moved down to Houston where the real estate market was exploding in 1982 and I joined the consulting firm of Kenneth Leventhal, which specializes in real estate. My intent was to spend several years learning the accounting and finance side of the business, then join a developer to learn the construction side. In September 1984, exactly two years after I arrived in Houston, I joined a developer to be his chief financial officer. He was a typical Houston developer—poor accounting records, shoot-from-the-hip style, with three or four projects going at the same time—an ex-banker who had become a developer. It's kind of an odd story.

My first assignment was to put the financials together for a board of directors meeting. After about six weeks of working through the shoeboxes and assembling a set of books and records, I finished an hour before the scheduled meeting. As I passed around the financial statements, I can remember the look of anticipation on everyone's faces. When they asked me to present the financial status of the company to them, I said, "Well, according to generally accepted accounting principles, you're broke."

Three weeks later the gentleman committed suicide in his house. I should have realized that this was a sign of a sure market top in the real estate market. It's a story of calamities that got progressively worse.

DORSEY: Where did you go from there?

BOWERS: I decided to try equipment leasing. The concept was simple: raise money from investors who purchased computer equipment and lease it to Fortune 500 companies. The purchase was highly leveraged, so between the depreciation and investment tax credit, the investors received big write-offs against their personal taxes.

It was a great concept, but bad timing. I started my own broker dealer firm in September 1985 to market these equipment leasing private placements. It took me until August 1986 before I had all the pieces in order to make my first sale. It was very well received, but in October 1986, the government passed the Tax Reform Act of 1986. That legislation eliminated all of the tax benefits of these transactions—so it was back to the drawing board for me.

DORSEY: What was your next venture?

BOWERS: I was living in Houston, the energy capital of the world. If you recall, in 1987 oil was $10 per barrel and natural gas was selling for $1 per mcf. So I thought that I would get into the business when it was at the bottom of the cycle instead of the top. I raised several million dollars from investors and struck out looking for a venture capital partner. I found a willing partner with Borden's, the milk company, which owned a small energy company it started in Louisiana to provide natural gas to its chemical and plastics division. Borden's owned a lot of acreage in Louisiana but had no money allocated for drilling because prices had dropped so low. It was a good combination, because the company's acreage had good shallow gas potential.

The only problem was that the attorney for the investors decided to keep the money that I had raised in escrow with a local trust company, which eventually became the first bankrupt trust company in the state of Texas about eight months into the drilling project. So what could have been a substantial annuity coming in every month from my percentage interest in the oil and gas wells, actually became little more than rent money by the time I paid all the contractors. But the common thread in all these stories is that I like to raise money. I like to put deals together. It was something I felt comfortable with.

After going from real estate to equipment leasing to oil and gas, I was ready to look for something a lot more stable. I had just gotten married. A baby was on the way. A friend suggested that, based on my background, I should look at being a stockbroker.

After interviewing at the major brokerage firms, someone suggested Lehman Bothers. I visited their office, and what I observed there were sixty brokers, all operating in fourth gear, working the phones hard, with no partitions, no walls, no offices, and just one big open boardroom. I could see from all this energy and excitement that if I was going to build a business, this was the best place to do it. So I set my sights on joining Lehman Brothers.

Lehman Brothers wasn't a place that hired inexperienced stockbrokers because they had no broker training program. Its strategy was to take a hard working, licensed broker with a year or two of experience at another firm, and teach them its way of doing business—stock picking combined with a very strong work ethic. The system used by Lehman Brothers was designed for ambitious and aggressive brokers. If you followed that system and worked hard, you could be very successful. I was very lucky to convince them to give me a try.

DORSEY: So they took a chance with you?

BOWERS: Well, getting hired was not easy. I went to Lehman's office in Houston every day, announced my presence, and waited in the lobby. I sat there doing paperwork on my other deals and I let the manager know that if he wanted to meet with me I was available and waiting.

After about three or four days of this, he invited me in and suggested I meet with the head of retail operations. I came back the next day to meet with this gentleman, who did his best to dissuade me. He saw me as a CPA who might have a problem with rejection. I turned him around, convinced him to give me a try, and in January 1990, I started working for Lehman Brothers for a very small monthly draw to start.

They put me in a boardroom with the other brokers, in the back, as far away as I could possibly be. Everyone was so intent on doing their own business that there was really no room for anyone to pull me aside and help me. I floundered for a long time without any assistance, but all I was focused on was opening accounts—and I did.

DORSEY: You couldn't have gotten into the market at a worse time—January 1990. But getting hired does show that perseverance pays off. Often times it takes a relentless campaign to get hired. I think in this business that is exactly what gets the attention of a branch manager. Sending out a résumé is not always the way to do it—camping on the doorstep of the branch manager's office may be.

BOWERS: I was persistent. The ironic thing about opening a lot of accounts in 1990 was that I was selling municipal bonds when interest rates were still high and others were promoting stocks. But I was opening up dialogue with high-net-worth individuals who bought municipal bonds, and when the stock market became more favorable towards equities, I already had an established relationship. It was a much easier sell than a cold call.

But as you know, opening accounts selling municipal bonds is not a very lucrative business, so in my first twelve months of production in 1990, I was probably the lowest producer in the firm's history.

DORSEY: How did you manage to keep the job?

BOWERS: My manager was about to send me packing. I remember sitting in his office looking at him. Before he could say anything, I said, "If I were sitting in your shoes, I would probably feel the same way. But please, I'm going to ask you not to, because if you fire me now, you're selling me at the bottom." He just rolled his eyes and told me to get back out there.

I began opening up a lot of new accounts and establishing new relationships each month. In 1991, I started to purchase junk bonds, which were trading at steep discounts and their yields were very high. My municipal bond clients purchased some of the higher-yielding bonds and they turned out very well. The credit market turned positive when interest rates declined, and what was junk in 1991 was being called "high yield" in 1995–97. The bonds appreciated considerably, and from there it was an easy transition from the high-yield bonds into equities.

That was how I made the transition. I attempted to learn as much as I could about a handful of stocks and to build large positions. That was how I became a large producer. It was a very commonsense approach to the business.

I also became a student of the business, and as I learned more, I formulated my own investment style, which was to take a top-down approach, beginning with an overall opinion about the economy and which industry sectors should benefit from certain economic events. Lehman Brothers had the number-one rated research department at the time, and its market strategist had made several very accurate calls, such as the October 1987 decline and the stock market surge in 1991, so we were receiving a lot of very favorable publicity. It was a great place to begin my career.

DORSEY: Tell me how you managed portfolios and positions then, as opposed to how you manage them now.

BOWERS: In 1992 banks were taking a lot of write-offs, most of which were non-cash write-offs because of bad real estate and other loans. I felt we were near the end of that cycle. I believed that with an interest rate decline, these stocks would likely bottom and reverse up, resulting in big upward movements. That is exactly what happened.

> *"I prefer to meet and become more familiar with my clients and their individual needs. . . this is primarily a service business and my clients expect and receive the highest quality of service I can offer."*
>
> SCOTT BOWERS

If I had been watching the technical indicators, I would have waited until January 1993 for a buy signal. For instance, I started recommending a bank stock in August 1992 at about $15 to $16. It went to about $16½ to $17, and then it slowly started to decline. By December, the stock declined to $10 and before the month was over, after the year-end window dressing, the stock had declined to a bottom of $8.50. I was hoping that there would not be any write-offs in the fourth quarter ending December 31. When the company reported a small profit in January, the stock jumped to $16 and ended upward of $30 by the end of 1993. That was the first stock that I had built a large position in, and when it took off, I went from being one of the lowest producing brokers to one of the top producers by using this sector rotation method.

DORSEY: I love to hear stories like this because it shows other brokers that it is possible to come back from a slump.

BOWERS: Ironically, at the end of 1990, I can recall going to my manager asking him if it was really possible to make a living in this business. Every stock I bought went down. I just couldn't see how this thing worked. But I stayed the course, continued to open new accounts and build large stock positions in companies that I had thoroughly researched and believed in—and it all came together for me in 1993.

DORSEY: You used the phone as your main prospecting tool?

BOWERS: Yes. As a matter of fact, that was the only thing I knew and I thought that was the only way to do it. In 1994, the equity markets were a little rougher. When you have large positions and you're wrong about what sectors are going to benefit, the going gets tough. At that time, I was only using fundamental analysis, and that is only half of the equation. It was a hard lesson to learn, but that was my introduction to technical analysis and its value. I learned that the two disciplines, when combined, form a very powerful team.

Soliciting stocks over the phone is much more difficult today because research is readily available and individuals are much more sophisticated. What clients need now is a broker who can help them solve their financial, retirement, and estate problems.

When Lehman Brothers decided to close their retail Houston branch in 1995, I joined PaineWebber. The environment at PaineWebber was much different. They took a broader approach to doing business. They wanted me to use my experience to assist clients in solving their financial problems, so I began doing seminars promoting PaineWebber's Portfolio Management Program, where I could personally manage the account, using a fee-based system.

I also started to rely heavily on using technical analysis combined with fundamental analysis. I was introduced to the Point and Figure system at PaineWebber, which has helped increase the performance in my clients' accounts. I always start with the fundamentals, but before I commit my clients' money, I always check to make sure the technicals are not giving me a different signal.

I now focus primarily on making sure my clients have their financial affairs and their estates in order. And although I don't give tax or legal advice, I work closely with PaineWebber's network of estate attorneys and the CPAs. I work through the Houston Chapter of CPAs, where I am the chairman of the Financial Planning Committee and on the board of directors.

Today, I prefer to meet and become more familiar with my clients and their individual needs. After all, this is primarily a service business and my clients expect and receive the highest quality of service I can offer.

DORSEY: Do you think that working with the CPAs is something most brokers can do, or is this something that's part of your work because you have that CPA designation? Would it be difficult for a non-CPA to work with a CPA?

BOWERS: It is probably one of the most difficult approaches you can take. It may take a long time to gain the CPAs' confidence so they feel comfortable enough to share their clients. I spent six years in public accounting and I know the language and CPAs' concerns, so this helps me work closely with them. Also, my involvement with the Houston chapter of CPAs exposes me to these professionals and their needs. They benefit, too, because they maintain control of their relationship with the client.

CPAs can provide financial, retirement, and estate planning services to their clients. The problem is, they are so inundated with their normal day-to-day work of taxes and audits, that it's very difficult—if not impossible—for them to also stay abreast of what's happening on my side of the business. I assist them in the areas that I focus on, and together we complete the job.

DORSEY: What type of products might you provide to the client that bridges the gap between you and the CPA?

BOWERS: My first step is to prepare a complementary financial and estate plan review. I have never had a review where there weren't areas that we could make constructive suggestions and improvements. I then make sure that the client is taking full advantage of everything that is available to him to maximize his estate and minimize his estate taxes. Next, the assets are identified and brokerage accounts that need to be consolidated are uncovered. Best of all, goodwill is established and relationships begin.

DORSEY: If it's determined that this client needs insurance in some form, are you able to go to a professional at PaineWebber who concentrates on insurance?

BOWERS: I am licensed to sell insurance and it is part of my business, but we also have a network of insurance wholesalers who are independent of PaineWebber. They are there to help us identify the best and most cost-effective insurance products and companies to use to make recommendations.

> *"I believe that the real future for new brokers is knowing how to. . .construct a financial framework for their clients based on their individual needs. It's about helping to protect assets for your clients."*
>
> SCOTT BOWERS

DORSEY: Do you think it is a good idea for brokers to use outside money managers?

BOWERS: It's very obvious that transaction-oriented business is becoming a commodity, and we are seeing more and more pricing pressure. I believe this same thing will happen in the wrap fee business. I believe what's going to happen is as the margins get smaller, it's going to require brokers to raise more and more money. So, I believe it will get tougher. But professional money management makes sense for some clients.

DORSEY: Scott, you talked about how you made the change from prospecting by phone to meeting with individuals face-to-face, and about your seminars with CPAs. What has this done for your business and how would you recommend that a broker conduct a seminar?

BOWERS: After coming to PaineWebber from Lehman Brothers, I tried to conduct seminars by contacting individuals directly. I found by doing a cost-benefit analysis of the amount of time, effort, and cost that went into attracting people, that this was definitely not the most effective way to do it. My current approach to seminars involves working with a team of outside professionals to put on a joint seminar with the CPA firms. The CPAs know which clients should attend. These clients feel the seminar will be beneficial to them and this adds a lot of credibility to our efforts. They are motivated to attend and to participate when their trusted CPA encourages them to attend.

DORSEY: If I'm not mistaken, PaineWebber is now hiring a lot of new trainees, as are many firms on Wall Street. Judging from the past, that's meant a top almost every time, when Wall Street starts hiring quickly. What do you see happening to the new brokers who are coming in today, the brokers who are just starting off after the market has been going up 30+ percent now for the past few years? How will the new brokers fare?

BOWERS: We are close to the peak in the number of people on Wall Street. For a new broker getting into the business right now, I would suggest they spend a long time getting educated in the business. They may have a much tougher road than I did when I got into the business. I'd advise new brokers to be prepared to go for a long period of time making very little money unless they have a lot of current relationships to use as a base.

It's difficult to open a lot of equity accounts now because the bull market has allowed amateurs to pick stocks as well as the professionals. I think the new brokers have to pick an area to concentrate on and they are going to have to work very hard to carve out that niche, because the business is becoming much more concentrated. When I started in the business, I was selling stocks and bonds. Then the fee-based system was popular. Now there is estate planning services and Rule 144. There are a lot of different ways that you can go in this business. But trying to do it all will be difficult.

I believe that the real future for new brokers is knowing how to solve their clients' financial problems and construct a financial framework for their clients based on their individual needs. It's about helping to protect assets for your clients, because that's their main objective. They'll need to be well versed in technical and fundamental analysis, as well as asset allocation, portfolio construction, and estate planning.

R. SCOTT BOWERS is a Senior Vice President of Investments and a member of PaineWebber's Portfolio Management Program. He currently serves his clients as part of the Emery Financial Group in Houston, Texas. He has an MBA from Long Island University and has held positions at Lehman Brothers, Price Waterhouse, and Kenneth Leventhal.

Samuel W. Lee, Salomon Smith Barney Inc.
Richmond, Virginia

SAM AND I HAVE BEEN friends for twenty-four years. I've always admired his deftness in maneuvering in questionable markets and coming out ahead. I became a broker at the end of the bear market of 1973–74. Sam was already in business at that time. He has made it through bull and bear markets, and every type of boom-and-bust climate: tax shelters, "no-lose" real estate deals, "no-risk" government bond funds, and just about everything else you can throw at a broker. He's built a solid business that continues to grow, and I am willing to bet that he will exceed forty years in the business before he retires.

Sam has found an interesting niche that I have not seen many brokers become involved in. He uses asset allocation to develop and manage his business. Where Sam differs from the typical "managed money" broker is that Sam maintains control of whether the funds are in or out of the market. The manager does the stock selection, Sam does the asset allocation. In this interview, Sam discusses what it was like to go through the 1973–74 bear market, and how he uses his niche to set himself apart from other brokers.

TOM DORSEY: When I first started in the business, you were already considered a seasoned broker. Your business has taken a number of turns over the years. Let's start with the bear market of 1973–74. Tell me about what it was like to operate as a stockbroker in those days.

SAM LEE: I entered the business in 1969. When I started out as a rookie, many of the brokers in my office were "First Family of Virginia" types, the blue-bloods that had ready-made business managing their own money and the family money. I didn't understand why they had hired me because I didn't have contacts, and my family didn't have money.

In 1969 my firm approved the sale of mutual funds. They had been around for a few years, but my firm wouldn't let brokers sell them because they felt that we could do a better job than a mutual fund manager. Then in 1973–74 the market topped out and began a decline of 50 percent that lasted a year and a half.

A few times we thought the decline was over, so we would buy stocks aggressively, and then the market would drop another 10 percent.

DORSEY: What would make you think it was over? Were there any indicators used, or was it just the 10 percent drop that signaled a bottom?

LEE: We had seen the corrections of 1968–69, which was a 15 percent correction. The greater the decline went, the closer we felt the bottom was. There was another factor, too—we simply wanted to do business. We were overly aggressive in trying to find the bottom, and we had never experienced losses like that before. Many brokers today have no idea how devastating a protracted bear market can be. It just destroyed your confidence. There were times when we felt every client hated us.

My wife would make my sandwiches each day and I'd eat at my desk. We had a management change in our office, and the new manager took my parking space away and moved me to another desk because he thought it was in too prestigious a location for a producer in the fifth quintile. I had gone from second quintile to fifth quintile. It wasn't a matter of laziness—there simply wasn't any business to do.

So I rode the bus. My net worth was probably $2,000, and I lost all of that. I didn't have two nickels to rub together, as they say. But the market got better, as it usually does.

DORSEY: Your specialty now is asset allocation. How do you manage your business?

LEE: I think that the way to stay in this business for twenty-nine years is to find the right style of business. In the '70s, I got into the gold phase. I made a lot of money in gold and thought it could never end. In the late '70s and early '80s, I got into limited partnerships, which was a mistake. I've made mistakes, but I've learned from them all and have become a much stronger broker because of it.

About eight years ago, I started to match clients' needs with the right professional money manager. I used outside services to determine when to be aggressive in the market and when to be conservative. I try to evaluate the risk in the market, and when the risk gets high and these services that I use start flashing warning signals, I lighten up in the market.

> *"The value that I'm adding for my clients is that I attempt to hit close to the S&P 500, but they are not in the market the whole year, to help reduce the risk level, which may be less than being fully invested."*
>
> SAM LEE

DORSEY: You are taking a customer's money and placing it with a money manager? What do you do when the risk gets high in the market?

LEE: The appropriate strategy would be to move the clients' funds to the manager's money fund—a mutual fund, for instance. We are currently in the large S&P 500 sector, and lately, that's outperformed the Russel 2000 by almost 15 percent.

DORSEY: How do you market the program?

LEE: I tend to think long term. Most of my marketing is done by referral. The managers have the performance, and then I use asset allocation. I've got very conservative money that has gone into the market that wouldn't have without my asset allocation strategy. My clients expect me to have the ability to be out of the market during a crisis.

DORSEY: The value added is that you manage the market and sector risk. The vast majority of risk in a stock is the market and sector risk.

LEE: The value that I'm adding for my clients is that I attempt to hit close to the S&P 500, but they are not in the market the whole year, to help reduce the risk level, which may be less than being fully invested. We don't apply the sharp's ratio to it to get a risk-adjusted return. We're more straightforward with it.

DORSEY: Do you know of anyone else using this strategy?

LEE: I'm the only one that I know of. Wall Street is so convinced that the "buy and hold" method is the only one. Offense is not always the best strategy. Of course, earlier in my brokerage career it was, but I have realized that defense is often the right course of action.

DORSEY: Relative to the total number of brokers practicing today, few have ever seen a true bear market. I think you may spark the interest in brokers to consider the asset allocation method of developing and managing their business. Sam, thank you very much for sharing your strategy.

SAMUEL W. LEE is First Vice President and Financial Consultant at Salomon Smith Barney. He joined the investment profession in October 1969 and has held positions at Merrill Lynch and Prudential. He specializes in monitoring and searching for professional money managers, and retirement and estate planning. A graduate of Virginia Tech, he currently sits on the University's Board of Advisors and is active in his local community.

CHAPTER 6

STARTING YOUR OWN FIRM

I HAVE ALWAYS BEEN a firm believer in that old cliché, "you only go around once in life." I think of this phrase as a directional for my life. I realized early on in my career that I wanted to run my own company. I had specific ideas about business that I felt were right, but I was unable to implement them at a larger firm.

Brokers are a fiercely independent lot, especially in today's environment. I think most brokers consider starting their own shop because the freedom is so alluring. A few decades ago, the possibility of starting one's own brokerage operation was slim. Without today's technology it was impossible to compete with the broker-dealers.

But now all firms are basically the same; the only difference between them is that the discounters usually have the same products, better technology, and lower fees.

Many firms have followed the example of the Raymond James' franchises. The franchise divisions have been in existence at Raymond James for decades, but only now are they being duplicated at other firms. The idea is to give independent brokers a shot at building a business of their own. The home office simply clears trades and manages back office operations. In return, brokers pay about 20 percent of their fees or commission for the service of the clearing agent. It's an attractive business model and it can be a great deal for both broker and clearing agent.

I selected two top brokers whom I have known for a number of years to interview for this chapter. One, Tim Daly, found it extremely easy to start his own operation. The most important thing, he maintains, is being Internet savvy. He even has an agreement with a competitor to assist his clients when he is away on vacation or on a business trips. He reciprocates when she is traveling. They live in different states, but that doesn't matter to their clients. Tim tells us how he made the successful leap to independence.

Another broker, Robert Cluck, describes the challenges and surprises he experienced in starting his own operation. He points out that not everyone is cut out to be an entrepreneur. These two viewpoints present a realistic picture of what it takes to go solo.

INTERVIEW

Robert Cluck, The Aspen Equity Group
Aspen, Colorado

I FIRST MET BOBBY at Dorsey, Wright's Stockbroker Institute in Richmond, Virginia. Today he runs a very successful brokerage operation in Aspen, Colorado, called The Aspen Equity Group.

Bobby has some interesting things to say about starting your own operation. He maintains that going solo has some mighty challenges, but his success may serve as inspiration to those of you who are ready to go out on your own.

TOM DORSEY: Let's just begin with your experience as a broker and how you got into the full-service business.

ROBERT CLUCK: I've been in the business for eleven years. I started on the institutional side for an investment-banking group in Houston, and I traded bonds for foundations, nonprofit groups, some smaller corporations, and some high-net-worth individuals. I focused on mortgage-backed securities. After two years of experiencing the trading floor and working with a very impersonal clientele, I decided that I wanted a radical change.

I went to Colorado to become a ski bum and decided to do whatever it took to get by. I also wanted to do some volunteer work with an organization called Young Life, which is a ministry that reaches out to high school students. So I ended up living with a couple of college buddies, planning to take a little time off to plan my next move and to become a human again.

I was working several jobs to pay the comparatively high living expenses in Aspen when one of the guys on our Young Life committee offered me a job. He owned a small independent broker-dealership and asked me to work with him. I accepted, but I hadn't done any business in a while, so I had completely lost the book that I had developed over two years. We had no technology and worked out of an index card file. I introduced myself to different people in this area and also retained some contacts from Texas, and that eventually grew into my retail base.

DORSEY: So when you started out on your own, the Internet was not in existence yet?

CLUCK: No Internet at all, and we shared a quote system on one PC that crashed frequently. The technology we had at Houston was isolated on the trading desk. After just half a year, our small broker-dealer merged with another, and we became a larger organization that represented a big fraction of folks in Colorado. But the three partners at my firm had different agendas and eventually decided that they couldn't work together any longer. They were going to close up shop.

I felt like I had just been kicked in the gut. I was tired of moving from place to place and having to explain that to my clients. I decided I was going to go out on my own and never a look back.

DORSEY: That's what did it for you?

CLUCK: Yes. I didn't want to work for anybody else again. But I needed to have a broker-dealer affiliate to be able to transact business, so I established both an RIA (registered investment advisor) and a broker-dealer affiliation. I kept my RIA and that is what I hung on the front door—my shingle, if you will—but at the bottom of the letterhead you would see that the securities were transacted through this broker-dealer based out of California. They were a full-service shop that serviced brokers across the country. And it was a fine arrangement. They allowed me to get on my feet and build a business. You have a larger percent payout than normal as you are picking up all your expenses. Just about every penny I had I poured back into what I considered my own business.

DORSEY: Did you succeed?

CLUCK: I worked as a registered investment advisor for a few years, and it probably would have continued longer, but the NASD and the SEC were particular about trying to keep a division between the discretionary investment advisers and broker-dealers. The clearing organization in California wanted me to give up my RIA, and I didn't want to do that. So we parted ways.

That's when I found Fidelity Investment Advisor Group. It's completely autonomous from any broker-dealer affiliate. I work completely on a fee structure, not on commissions. And I have an asset-under-management contract with all of my clients that allows me to have limited power of attorney to manager their accounts, so they are all discretionary. I do not have to call a client when I have an idea, I can simply manage the money as I choose. This allows me to focus on the relationship with the clients, because if they are going to give me that kind of power, I need to know what they want to do. I reduced my client base, and now I can spend more time talking to my customers about their financial goals. The number of accounts I manage has decreased, but my income has increased.

> *"After just half a year, our small broker-dealer merged with another. . .I decided I was going to go out on my own and never a look back. "*
>
> ROBERT CLUCK

DORSEY: So in essence you kept the high-net-worth customer?

CLUCK: Yes, the 80-20 rule. Where 80 percent of your business typically comes from 20 percent of your clients. This way there is no conflict of interest because I am not taking on new clients just to earn a larger commission. Knowing exactly what is coming in each month helps to manage my business. I am able to invest in my business each month to provide better technology and services for my clients by knowing exactly what the revenue stream is.

DORSEY: When you are working on a fee basis, in some cases the right investment is none at all. That is, sometimes you have to just sit tight and not make any transactions.

CLUCK: Right. For example, in the recent bull market, I was able to substantially increase my clients' holdings in cash. I looked at all of their positions, and decided whether to hold, trim back, or whatever was necessary without having to increase the customer's costs.

It's hard for clients who are used to transaction-oriented business to get used to this fee arrangement. I believe that it will eventually become the norm, because clients don't want to pay large commissions every time the broker has to make a decision. The value-added service we are providing right now, which we didn't have the time to do before, will also remain intact in a bear market. So I am able to pay more attention to the clients, and it has been good for them and also increased revenues to my firm.

> *"When you are working on a fee basis, in some cases the right investment is none at all. That is, sometimes you have to just sit tight and not make any transactions."*
>
> THOMAS DORSEY

DORSEY: Tell me about the costs of getting started. We've talked about this before, and I know it's much more difficult to go out on your own than most people think. Many brokers are wooed by the higher payout without thinking about the hidden costs of paying all the expenses yourself.

CLUCK: I would completely skip the independent broker situation. I would go straight to a registered investment advisor designation.

DORSEY: Why wouldn't the broker just keep the same continuity of business as a stockbroker and just go on his own and clear through a clearing broker-dealer?

CLUCK: I have more autonomy as an RIA. I can make clearing arrangements with broker-dealers. I can get all different types of research from various sources—but I'm not tied to one broker-dealer as I might be if I took the independent brokerage direction.

I call it "grazing." It's as if I can graze on all kinds of different ranch land. I can go for the best grass. I'm not restricted to one pastureland. For example, I can use a certain wirehouse's research or collect it over the Internet. If I want to have my own filtering process, I can use a number of different research tools and filter them through my own in-house system. I'm able to collect research from sources other than my own house. There are so many built-in conflicts of interest in investment bank relationships that in-house research should be viewed with a skeptical eye.

DORSEY: What has the Internet done for your business?

CLUCK: I feel much more confident in my ability to manage clients' assets. It's not just because of the convenience. I'm looking at it from an operational standpoint. Through the Internet, I can be completely up-to-date on every activity that's going on with all my clients.

Before the proliferation of technology, a client might call up asking where his dividend was and I wouldn't even be aware he was owed one because we didn't have the technology to stay abreast. Today, however, I can log onto my system and see exactly how many assets I have under management and be warned of any odd-lot tenders, splits, or rights offerings. In the past, a client would call with a question about what he should do with the rights offering, and I didn't even know the offering had taken place.

DORSEY: That's got to be a strange feeling when a customer calls with more information than you have.

CLUCK: Frankly, I'm not really that threatened by it because the corporate strategy I've established for this company allows us to focus on our main clients. We want to empower our clients and help them take control of their investment endeavors. It might eventually result in our educating them enough that they could do it themselves, but that is the risk we are willing to take. We want our clients to know that we are looking after their best interests.

DORSEY: What type of prospecting do you do now that you are on your own? How do you open new accounts?

CLUCK: For better or for worse, we have not done any active prospecting for years. Our clients have come to us strictly by referral. I have chosen to pour my energies into servicing the clientele that has stuck with me. I don't make time to look for new business, and that might be a fault. I'm not concerned with becoming a huge money management firm; I would rather have quality of life. I really enjoy my business. It's a manageable size and it's a manageable pace. It's almost anti-prospecting rather than actively prospecting. We rarely do any workshops, unless it's by invitation, where a company has asked us to come in and do a presentation. I haven't had a business card in two years.

This business is built solely on relationships. I'm trying to build my niche by providing service, maintaining contact between my clients and myself, and being very discreet. Because I live in a small community where people know other peoples' business, we don't even have a sign on our front door. I think the exclusivity of what we do tends to attract high-net-worth clients. So, if somebody drops in to establish an account, I take a hard look at whether it's likely to be a viable relationship. We don't necessarily have to be close friends, but I have to have an understanding of how they want to do business.

DORSEY: So, if someone walked in the door and expressed an interest in plotting some complicated or overly risky day trading maneuvers, you probably wouldn't take the account?

CLUCK: No, I would give him E-Trade's number and say, "Go for it."

DORSEY: Tell me about your staff. How is the office environment structured?

CLUCK: No one has an office. All of the programs on all the computers are the same. We have a trading room where I sit with my assistant, and we have all of the information we need to manage these accounts within two steps of the trading desk.

We spend most of our time in the trading room, and we also have the conference room, lounge room, and a general reception area. It is designed to be very fluid. There is no feeling of a hierarchy—we just work together as a team. The downside of operating your own business is that you really don't know what a vacation is. Where I live, the ski lifts close on April 5, and people shut down their businesses. Restaurants are closed down. And there is not a big professional community here in Aspen. That kind of compounds the vacation problem even more—sometimes it seems like we're the only ones working.

DORSEY: Yes, the market never stops. But it's not exactly a hardship living in Aspen, Colorado.

CLUCK: No, you're right. But this business really has to be in your blood. You have to think about it all the time and have passion for it; it's not just something you do for a living. I think very few people are cut out to do this type of work. It's hard on relationships, hard on the people that you really love. Unless you are really committed, you had better choose to do something else.

DORSEY: Do you have any other money managers with you?

CLUCK: No. But I may add a co-portfolio manager.

DORSEY: I have known you for years, Bobby, and you have come a long way. So I think one of the main points that you have made in this conversation is that if a broker wants to start out on his own, he or she should bypass the brokerage side and go right into being a registered investment advisor. Becoming a registered investment advisor puts you in a different type of field, and allows you to work with brokers, too, if you need to.

CLUCK: Yes. But you also have to be committed to the technology or you won't make it. You must invest a significant amount of your gross into technology. Being an entrepreneur in this business is very different from working for a large firm. It's gone very well for us. Our assets under management have increased significantly. I live by the words that Shakespeare wrote in *Hamlet,* "To thine own self be true."

I would strongly suggest that people considering a career change away from the corporate environment take a personality test with a company like Myers Briggs that would tell them how well they would do on their own. In this environment you must be both the president and the janitor.

> *"If you don't have . . . a personality that can withstand the hardships of going it alone, you're only kidding yourself. "*
>
> ROBERT CLUCK

DORSEY: That is exactly right. I know what it is like to take my own trash out and to vacuum the floor myself.

CLUCK: Yes, you dust your own desktops and do your own filing when you're just starting out. You have to negotiate things for the back office, fiddle with your computers endlessly, and you have to learn to be a master at it all. You need to know if it is better to lease a copier or buy it, and what's the best deal on long distance phone service. That's too many decisions for some people.

DORSEY: That's right. But when it's all for you and your business these things are enjoyable.

CLUCK: It's not all drudgery, you're right. But it's a lot of decision-making time that takes away from your real purpose for being there.

DORSEY: So not everyone is capable or even wants to lead?

CLUCK: Oh, sure. We are all different, no question about it, because you have to be entrepreneurial, and not everyone is prepared to go out and take the risks of starting a venture on their own by any stretch of the imagination. Most good brokers that I know at brokerage firms probably should be there, and for good reason. They have to focus on only one thing—being the best they can at the investment process. Managing a business is much different.

I went down a lot of blind alleys and made some mistakes, learned from them, got back on my feet, dusted off my pants, and kept going. But I think there are some guys who need to stay where they are. If you don't have a supportive relationship at home or a personality that can withstand the hardships of going it alone, you're only kidding yourself.

DORSEY: Very good advice. Thanks, Bobby. Good luck to you in the future. I'll be following you.

> ROBERT L. CLUCK, CFP, is a registered investment advisor who lives and works in Aspen, Colorado. After graduating from Baylor University, he began his career in 1987 as a bond trader in Houston, Texas, for an institutional firm. Next, he became part of a small broker-dealer firm in the Rockies and then moved on to become an independent advisor when that partnership dissolved. He has run The Aspen Equity Group since 1992.

Timothy J. Daly, The Weston Group, Inc.
Weston, Connecticut

I MET TIM DALY when he was a broker at a major wirehouse located in Connecticut. He's been on his own for several years now, and he uses Internet technology to set up an interesting arrangement for support from a fellow broker.

Without the advent of the Internet, going it alone would not have been possible. One of the most important services a major firm provides its brokers is research. That research is now free anywhere on the Internet one chooses to go. One more major roadblock that has in the past prohibited brokers from starting their own brokerage shop was back office operations. Now with the Internet, that task is easily accomplished. Tim has found that being computer literate has been a major contributor to his success. If a branch's special dynamics incorporated a team-working atmosphere, you can still achieve this over the Internet via chat rooms and other online discussions, not to mention e-mail.

For instance at Dorsey, Wright & Assoc. our two portfolio managers are stationed in California, while the home office is located in Richmond, Virginia. Ten years ago that would not have been possible. Because of technology, today it's as if our money managers reside in an office next door. Tim has been able to work effectively with this new technology. Technology is only going to increase the possibilities for going it alone in the future. Vacations are a breeze now, all you need is a laptop and an electric plug and you can access your clients' status reports from your firm's back office; you can also stay in touch with your clients via e-mail. Who says an office has to be defined as a geographic location? Five years from now, with video technology, it'll be like having a personal meeting with your client when each of you are on opposite coasts or in different countries.

TOM DORSEY: I would like to know a little bit about how you started in the business, so let's begin there.

TIM DALY: Sure. I started in 1986 right out of college with a degree in economics. I spotted an ad in *The Wall Street Journal* for an investment-banking job. As it turned out, it was essentially a bond broker's position with a small firm. They got me registered, taught me how to sell municipal and Ginnie Mae bonds to small institutions and individuals. I did that for about ten months and decided that being a bond broker in what seemed like a roaring bull market for stocks was limiting myself. We were not allowed to do stocks there. So I made a number of friends at another brokerage, Rothschild, and sold my way into there by telling the manager that I would be the best broker they had ever seen.

After telling me there were no positions available, they finally let me in the door. And that was sometime before August 1987.

DORSEY: The fateful year?

DALY: I think it was the best opportunity ever for a broker to start because I had very few accounts when the crash occurred. Virtually everybody out there was very unhappy with their broker. I spent the entire month bringing in new money, raising new accounts, and going out to make presentations to prospective clients. Almost every stock that I bought made money—Gillette, Anheuser-Busch, Polaroid. At that point it was easy. Everybody's accounts were up for sale, and I got as many as I possibly could.

The one problem with Rothschild was that on the day of the crash, it lost a very substantial amount of money in its own account in plain risk arbitrage, and the rumors became rampant that we were going out of business. It wasn't just Rothschild; many firms were rumored to go under. Sure enough, in March 1988 we were taken over by Oppenheimer & Company. And they promptly moved us down to the World Financial Center on the fifth-floor boardroom. That's when my real trading began.

The manager was an exceptional salesman. He taught us all the basics. He took our hard work and put it to really good use. With Oppenheimer, the motivation was good, and the management was excellent. Everything about Oppenheimer was working with the exception that it was a value-based research firm, and it just didn't click for me. I never quite had confidence that the research was comprehensive enough for me to make solid recommendations.

DORSEY: When you say value-based research, what you mean is that they bought fundamentally sound stocks that were down and out?

DALY: That's right. They were looking first fundamentally at the assets of the corporation, what the machinery was worth, what the business was worth, on a very conservative basis and then they were trying to buy it at a discount.

DORSEY: I actually like that type of research as long as the technical side also works.

DALY: I think that was good, too, and we did get some great names; we also bought a lot of great names that stayed very cheap for a long time and got a lot cheaper before they went higher. And as a relatively new broker, I can remember taking substantial positions in Fruit of the Loom, which was a great recommendation, and a company called Texas Air and Black & Decker, all around the same time. I had a lot of margin and the stocks kept on going lower and lower and lower. Texas Air was my biggest position at Oppenheimer at the time. The analysts at Oppenheimer reiterated the recommendation but the stock just kept going lower.

We margined to the absolute hilt and Texas Air eventually went out of business. So at that point I realized this perhaps was not the only way to evaluate equities. I started looking for other alternatives. I moved from Oppenheimer's downtown office to the midtown Manhattan office, following my previous branch manager. There I met an older broker who was deeply involved in technical analysis. At the time I couldn't understand the concept, so I bought a few books to read on the subject, followed what he said, and started to see that there was something to it. I remember a very popular phrase we used when we were pitching new accounts: "We like the stock because the chart pattern looks like the stairs in your house, it keeps on going up." And I was now starting to think on a more technical level. It wasn't until I left Oppenheimer and went to PaineWebber in Darien, Connecticut, that I started doing the Point and Figure method, with a man named Joe Davis.

Joe was so rabidly into Point and Figure that it was scary at first. He explained why the process was relevant. When looking at a bullish chart, we could initiate positions on pullbacks and get better risk parameters. And over the years I spent with PaineWebber, I learned the process.

"When you are your own boss, you make the decisions—the good decisions, and of course, the bad decisions."

TIM DALY

Since I was the most computer-literate person in the office, I took charge of downloading for the office. I set up a PC, put a modem in there and cleaned it up a bit, and every day I would make sure that it was online and doing what it was supposed to do.

I was absolutely convinced that you had to merge the fundamentals with the technicals. There was no doubt in my mind that the process worked, and if I hadn't learned how to use it, my ability to go out on my own would have been seriously hampered.

DORSEY: When did you first consider going solo?

DALY: At major wirehouses, there was a lot of pressure to do the in-house products. At one previous firm my former partner and I were the top two equity brokers in the office. A new manager was hired, and he changed the direction of the office. That was when I began to consider going it alone. A friend of mine from a major wirehouse had gone on her own and was very successful. She cleared with First Montauk Schroders & Company, set up her own firm and absolutely loved it—the independence, having the market herself for what she did best. After watching her for about a year, I decided that I was going to do it myself. Part of what made this a very easy move for me was that I have a solid foundation in how I manage my business. I know that the backbone of my firm is the way I fuse Point and Figure technical analysis with fundamental analysis, and I have access to virtually every analyst's report on the street, regardless of where it comes from.

I have contacts everywhere, but it's via the Internet. I get hard copy research and First Call research from Byron Schroder, and I use Schroders's research as well as Salomon Smith Barney. We are starting to get First Boston and Emerald Research, which is good for small-cap investing, and I also get other major wirehouse research. I have all the fundamental research I could ever hope for.

My fundamental research consists of second analyst briefs, and, of course, the reports on CNBC. I also have S&P 500, which has really sound research.

DORSEY: Tell me about the logistics of operating your own business. You made the decision to go out on your own. I assume you stayed right in your neighborhood.

DALY: Yes, just a few minutes away.

DORSEY: And you are clearing through Wortheim Schroder? How would a broker set up a clearing arrangement like that? What are the benefits of going out on your own?

DALY: When you are your own boss, you make the decisions—the good decisions, and of course, the bad decisions. So how well you do is based upon your effort, and that's the key. Most of us in this business work very hard. We work long hours, and we take a lot of pressure. But when you are giving away 40 percent or 50 percent of your commissions to the firm for research you can get elsewhere, it may not be worth it. You can do it just as easily yourself. There are a lot of packaged clearing arrangements available.

For example, you can go to First Montauk, and they will pay you a percentage of your commissions, help maintain the broker-dealership, maintain all those records, and the legal department, which deals with compliance. When you set up your own corporation, they pay everything directly to you, and you disburse the funds. Obviously, you have to be a registered principal and have your Series 24. You have to maintain certain records for a number of years, arrange for online access for your quotes and back office.

Being computer- and Internet-savvy is extremely important. With the advent of the Internet, it makes researching easy. S&P Comstock has a program that does much of it for you. I have live quotes, S&P fundamentals, and level 2 Nasdaq. I've got more information than I would ever want or need, and I pay S&P Comstock a very small monthly fee for that.

"I wear an awful lot of hats.
It's essentially me and the computers."

TIM DALY

DORSEY: Things have really changed. Only a few years ago getting a simple quote system would have been a major expense. Now real-time quotes are a commodity. What about customer statements? Does your customer get the same types of statements as when you operated at a major wirehouse?

DALY: Yes. The statements that the customer gets and the conformations are the standard Schroder statement. It will have the broker-dealer that you are using, and it's quality stuff. It's as if they have an account at Schroder with a representative working at that company. The customer's cash positions and stock positions are held at Schroder. You don't take possession of anything. And it's insured.

Schroder has the standard Pacific Insurance, and they have additional insurance through Aetna. One of the things I like about Schroder is the fact that it is a high-end organization. It says that it clears exclusively for institutional trading accounts, very large institutions, and the top broker-dealers. Many customers ask, "How do I know that you are not going to take any money and run?" I'm not keeping cash balances. Schroder is keeping all cash balances. It is maintaining all the insurance on the accounts.

DORSEY: When you take all the responsibilities of starting your own business, your payout increases dramatically, does it not?

DALY: It can be close to 90 percent depending on the deal you are able to arrange. I found an average of about 65 percent after I pay all my expenses. You are probably forgetting one of the most important things, and that is corporate structure. There are tax benefits to paying these expenses from a corporate entity.

DORSEY: How many clients came with you when you started your own business?

DALY: I didn't retain as many of my accounts as I thought I would, and I'm still in the process of bringing clients over. Most of my larger accounts came over the first week. The smaller accounts are the vulnerable ones. I'm still working on a number of them while opening new accounts every week. I just have to keep working hard.

DORSEY: When you develop new business now as an independent, do you meet with any resistance when you are prospecting or developing business, as opposed to when you were with a full-service firm?

DALY: I haven't met with much. When I do meet with it, one of the ways I combat it is to simply explain to them why I started my own company. There is nothing negative I have to say about any other firms. When it comes to the customer, there isn't much difference between being at a large wirehouse or clearing through Schroeder.

DORSEY: As far as staff is concerned, you are running this by yourself. Do you have any other brokers in the office?

DALY: I have started hiring brokers, the first about two months ago. He went through the training program at one of the major wire-houses. I would like to hire five brokers and have targeted those who have been in the business between one and three years, but don't have a game plan yet. I will promise to teach them the process I have used to manage accounts.

DORSEY: Do you have a secretary?

DALY: I did not bring a secretary over. I wanted to keep my costs as low as possible. So, I wear an awful lot of hats. It's essentially me and the computers. Remember, I'm very computer savvy so I am able to have them do much of the work for me. I have at my fingertips every bit of information about every one of my clients. On my screen I have live quotes, behind it I could have my Dorsey, Wright Web page, behind that I can have my Schroder & Company clearing service division software right into my account. At the click on a mouse button I can be into any one of them at a second's notice.

DORSEY: When you're out of the office, who watches over the business?

DALY: Remember the friend who inspired me to go out on my own? One of the reasons I chose to clear through Montauk and with Schroder was because she also was with them—we have access into each other's accounts. So, for example, for the month of December she went to Australia. Each of her clients had my phone number, and I had all of her clients' phone numbers. I knew all their positions, and I had access into her back office. So if anyone needed quotes or wanted to trade, they called me, and I handled it for her. It was just a matter of putting a different password into the software, and I was right into her account.

I actually took my first two-day vacation about two weeks ago, and it happened to be on a day when there was a lot of activity in the stocks I owned. A number of clients called, and she handled every inquiry and trade that needed to be done. If somebody called and left a message on voice mail, she returned a call promptly, and it was seamless. The client doesn't even know that she is in a different state. We are starting to do some teleconferences together, so we can split costs. I essentially have a backup broker. We schedule everything around each other. If she is going to be out, we schedule it in advance. She would call me from a dive boat in Australia on a cellular phone, and we would talk about some of the things that were done for her clients that day, and it was incredible.

The only drawback, of course, is that if you were running an office with other brokers, you have to supervise them; that's the one thing you have to keep in mind. If a new account is opened, someone who is a principal must sign off on it. It's important to think about having a backup principal available if you are going to hire other brokers to work for you.

> *"When the compliance people came here and saw what I had set up, they started taking photos and asking me questions. They couldn't believe what they saw."*
>
> TIM DALY

DORSEY: Where do you think this is all going? Do you think there are more brokers that are going to be going out on their own? What do you think the future holds here?

DALY: I think there are a lot of people who are interested in the brokerage business. I think you have to be entrepreneurial by nature. It's a major step that I think most brokers are not prepared to take. There will be many more who do, however.

It's a scary step the first time, as confident as you are of yourself and your abilities, but once you have made the step, you would probably not consider going back.

Before I even got my Series 7 transferred, there was a five-day period in which I had to pay another broker in a local office with a clearing firm to supervise me. When I went to meet this person for the first time, I walked into his office and I didn't see a computer anywhere, just phone and papers and things scattered all over. I think he managed about $5 million, most of it on a discretionary basis. And I asked him, "Where do you get your quotes from?" And he leaned over onto the floor and picked up yesterday's *Wall Street Journal*. He said, "Here is my quote system. This is all I need to have right here." He seemed to me to be very typical of a lot of the existing independent people. They just weren't savvy; they weren't up on the Internet. When the compliance people came here and saw what I had set up, they started taking photos and asking me questions. They couldn't believe what they saw. I happened to come in right on the cusp when the Internet was available.

So in essence there are two sets of brokers out on their own: the old guard who are still in the dark ages and have little technology, and the new guard who are technology- and Internet-savvy, who are state of the art.

DORSEY: Tim, thanks for the interview. This is great information for any broker interested in going it alone.

TIM DALY is the founder and president of The Weston Group, Inc., a full-service money-management, brokerage, and investment firm in Connecticut. The firm is affiliated with First Montauk Securities, Inc. and Schroder and Co. Tim has held numerous positions in finance, including associations with Morgan Stanley Dean Witter, PaineWebber, Oppenheimer, and LF Rothschild.

CHAPTER 7

BUILDING A PARTNERSHIP

AN OLD FRIEND OF MINE once said when I was consider-ing a partnership: "Tom, there is only one thing worse than a partnership, and that's a sinking ship." I went ahead anyway and got myself into a partnership, and he was right—the ship sank. I entered the alliance for the wrong reasons.

One wrong reason was money. It was during the tax-shelter craze. My new partner understood these products and was able to explain their complexities to investors. I thought becoming partners would be a good way to participate in this business since I was doing virtually no tax shelter work. The problem with tax shelters was that the product was flawed. People only bought them to get some sort of break on their taxes, and the underlying merits of the shelter were not important. Once the product broke down, so did the partnership. We didn't have other common goals to keep the alliance together.

I am now in the twelfth year of a successful partnership at Dorsey, Wright & Associates. My partner, Watson Wright, and I have different functions, but we complement one another. Our personalities are at opposite ends of the spectrum, but we have tremendous success working together. Watson is much more detail-oriented, and I concentrate on the big picture. Our three top analysts, Tammy Derosier, Susan Morrison, and Jay Ball, also run the company. In fact, Tammy is as much a part of the company's big picture as I am, and she is also as detail oriented as Watson. With Tammy, Sue, and Jay at the executive level of the company, we're as strong as ever. There is no weak link in this company. If something happened to Watson and me, they could step right in and run the company. I have never found it necessary to look at the company books or write a check, not once. That's how a partnership should be. Total loyalty, integrity, and trust between all partners and employees.

The mechanics of partnerships depend upon the structure of the company and how you plan to grow. We have chosen to grow slowly and with no debt except for $90,000 we borrowed to get started twelve years ago.

Profit can never be the only consideration when a partnership is formed. State your practical goals upfront and make sure your partner(s) share your objectives and can form a cohesive unit to help the company move in a positive direction. You must concentrate on producing the absolute best product or service you are able to provide. Once you have developed this approach and have properly implemented it, the money will come.

Treat your partnership as a living thing and you'll do well. The best way to communicate how to form a successful partnership is to look at some that have thrived. This chapter presents two partnerships that work.

Edward M. Rosenberg, David M. Rosenberg, & Richard H. Angelotti, Morgan Keegan & Co., Inc. Sarasota, Florida

I HAD THE PLEASURE of meeting Ed Rosenberg at our Stockbroker Institute in Richmond, Virginia. He is one of those brokers people seem to trust immediately. His partner is Richard Angelotti, a lawyer and former bank president. Also on the scene is Ed's son, David Rosenberg, a junior partner and the future of their business.

A funny thing happened to me the day I called Ed to arrange an interview time. I was in Venice, Florida, near where they operate. I had called his number and was waiting for his assistant to call him to the phone when I looked down at the open business section of the Sarasota newspaper. I couldn't believe what I read. The title of the article was "The Dynamic Duo," and there was Ed and Dick's picture in an article about their partnership. The article spanned about three pages and brought in about $19 million of new business for them. The partnership has about $385 million in assets, and it has continued to grow. They call it a marriage of different strengths and interests. If you are in a partnership or thinking about going into one, read on, because these guys do it right.

TOM DORSEY: Ed, let's talk about how you began in the business and how you and Dick eventually started a partnership.

ED ROSENBERG: I first became interested in the stock market when I was a young boy. I was 13 years old when I began investing, and I was pretty successful from the start. The first stock I ever bought was Xerox. I sold Xerox and bought Polaroid—and I nearly tripled my money on each. That sparked my interest in the market. After I finished school I came to Sarasota, but there was very little sophistication here in the investment community twenty-five years ago.

I got lucky and landed a job in a bank here. Because I was the only one with a financial background, I was given the job as portfolio manager. That's how I got started. I moved up in banking and eventually became president of the bank. I ran the portfolio while I was president. I had a broker's license, and in 1984 I started what was to become a very successful investment subsidiary in the bank. After the bank was sold in 1987, I got into the brokerage business. I went to work for Kidder Peabody, which was eventually sold to Merrill Lynch. Then I moved over to Smith Barney.

Finally, I came to work at Morgan Keegan. I had known Dick Angelotti for many years before that. We had different strengths. Dick is a great asset gatherer; he enjoys doing that. I prefer to manage portfolios as I have done for years. A kind of synergy developed between us, and we joined forces. I also took David, my son, as a partner when he graduated from school.

Since then, it's been a fruitful partnership. The pieces fit together. We all do our jobs, but we approach the same business from different angles.

DORSEY: Dick, would you please tell me how you gather assets?

DICK ANGELOTTI: I was a trust and tax attorney in Chicago from 1969 to 1982, and one of my largest clients was Northern Trust Bank. They were opening up an office in Sarasota, Florida, and they hired me to come down and help them get started. We went from nothing to $1.4 billion in trust assets in eight years. In Sarasota, bankers were wearing open shirts and sport coats and sponsoring golf tournaments. We came down here to determine where the money was in Sarasota. We found that it was in the arts, so we started sponsoring the ballet, symphony, art exhibits, and operas. We ended up dominating the marketplace.

In 1990, I was hired away to become the president of the Bank of Boston's Florida operation, which had offices in Miami, Sarasota, and Palm Beach. I did that for three years, and then was hired by a large broker-dealer which had a branch office in Sarasota.

In making that transition, I sat on the investment committee of both banks and learned to market that way, but I was not a stock selector. During my first six months, I had over $100 million in assets, but I really didn't know what to do with it. I was looking for outside money managers to help me, because in my role in both institutions I had focused on bringing assets into the bank and finding places to put them. We had investment counselors in the bank to render that kind of advice and to manage those assets.

Since I had known Ed and David for a number of years, I thought that we might be able to become partners. Ed was my kind of person. He had the same kind of close relationship with clients that I had. When Ed came over to join my firm as a broker, I saw the way he ran his business. I knew that he was the resource that I needed to handle the investing of the assets that I brought into the firm.

Our roles are well defined, although we overlap a little. Ed clearly picks the stocks and makes the timing and selections, but we consult on it. David and I are involved in that process, but not nearly as much as Ed is, and David is also involved in the asset-gathering end, as I have been. He has gotten out into the community and become well known. This is a marriage of different strengths and interests. Every client becomes a friend, and we are in constant contact with them.

Our results are as strong as anybody's on the street. When we first started together, I had been lining up outside money managers, not knowing that I would have an inside partner to deal with. When we opened a new account, we would give half of the assets to an outside money manager and give the other half to Ed to handle internally. Over the three years, Ed consistently beat every other money manager out there, in large part due to Point and Figure and also his own research and discipline. By the end of the third year, we had no accounts other than global ones with Brandes or Morgan Stanley in which we were using an outside manager.

DORSEY: Dick, how did you develop your asset-gathering abilities?

ANGELOTTI: I became very involved in the community. I sat on four or five boards at a time and learned who had money and who didn't. I got to know the players in the community. And I made a point to talk to these people about their investments and ask how we could help them. We have relationships with the top three or four estate planning attorneys in the community, and because our clients are happy with Ed's performance, they continue to refer friends to us.

> *"I don't think you have to retire from this business. This is something you can still do three days a week when you are seventy."*
>
> DICK ANGELOTTI

DORSEY: David, give me an idea of what part you play in the partnership.

DAVID ROSENBERG: Growing up with a father who was the president of a bank gave me some sophistication in finance. But I originally went to the University of Notre Dame to play football. I was planning to go into professional football, but I broke my leg, and that put a damper on things.

DORSEY: It looks like you found a pretty good career in spite of not going pro.

D. ROSENBERG: I found a great career. After I graduated from Notre Dame, I came down and worked with my dad at Smith Barney.

DORSEY: Did you work as a registered representative or did you work as someone's cold caller?

D. ROSENBERG: I worked as a registered representative developing my own business and my own book. Once I had passed the Series 7, I went to New York for sales training. I started out cold-calling investors. I worked hard at it. I was motivated by the thought that the next call I made could be huge. Here in Sarasota, with the financial resources people have, a prospect could buy a million dollars' worth of bonds right off the bat. I used bonds to open most of my new accounts. Bonds are typically boring compared to equities; however, you are not going to offend anybody by offering bonds. If it is an AAA tax-free Florida bond, it's all about yield and how you present it and yourself.

Things are changing rapidly in this business. I have the best of both worlds working with my father and Dick. I can watch my father manage money and take the best parts of that. I can also watch how Dick treats his clients with utmost respect, and how he gathers assets. If I can combine the best of both worlds, then I think I will have a very long-term career in the brokerage industry.

DORSEY: So you're a junior partner of sorts?

D. ROSENBERG: Since I am only 28, I've got at least another two or three years to work my way up.

DORSEY: It's great to have someone who can take over the business some day. At some point, Ed, you and Dick will want to take a less active role in the business.

E. ROSENBERG: We have always pictured David as our future, but he is also a huge part of our present. He has learned the investment end and does research for us. He has brought in a lot of assets and continues to do that. So he is a strong part of what we do today.

DORSEY: When I first started in the business, brokers never thought of a client base as proprietary business. When a broker retired, his book was simply split up amongst the other brokers. But today, you have to run the business as if it were all your own.

ANGELOTTI: If I were ready to slow down or retire, or Ed wanted to, there is continuity with David. We will be bringing in a couple of other people prior to our retirement, and it will be an ongoing organization that can support Ed and me in retirement. I don't think you have to retire from this business. This is something you can still do three days a week when you are seventy. It all comes down to having the right people to continue growing the business. That's the beauty of building a partnership.

DORSEY: Ed, explain the nuts and bolts of how you manage the accounts. If an individual comes in with $200,000 and wants to open an account with you, what do you do?

E. ROSENBERG: First, we want to gauge the potential clients' goals and objectives so that we know exactly where to put their money. We ask them to fill out a seven-page questionnaire to determine their needs. A lot of people come in not knowing what they want. They hope their money will grow, but they don't know if they want income. We look at people's asset composition, age, and the risks they are willing to take, and then we allocate the funds accordingly—and again, I have to stress, with the largest amount of money going into equities. And we use what's called "systematic withdrawal" from mutual funds or from the money that we manage. We don't talk about bonds because we are not really fixed-income oriented. There is a time to invest in bonds, but you can get more bang for your money in equities.

DORSEY: With modern medicine and longer life spans, a person has a real chance of outliving his nest egg.

E. ROSENBERG: We take that into consideration. We used to think that making $10,000 or $20,000 a year was a dream. And retirees who settled in Florida with $200,000 in cash used to think that they had it made. Those people now are hurting. Therefore, we explain to all of our clients that they need to have a growing income in order to keep pace with inflation and not outlive their money.

DORSEY: How would that work?

E. ROSENBERG: If a person comes in with half a million dollars and wants to generate income, we will allocate $40,000 a year, or 8 percent on the money, knowing that the market has averaged 12½ percent over the past seventy years. Every month we send the client 8 percent annualized, and at the end of the year we will re-examine where the person stands. We will never cut the amount of money that we give them, but we might increase it the following year based on the performance in the account. With the 30+ percent increases over the last couple of years, that 8 percent is 16 percent or more of the initial investment. Systematic withdrawal is the way to make your money work for you over a long period of time.

DORSEY: David, you're learning both sides of the equation here. Do you lean more toward asset gathering or stock management? At some time in the future, you are going to be running the show as your dad and Dick begin to phase out.

D. ROSENBERG: Dick has a son-in-law in this business, and I'm sure that we will wind up joining forces some day. But I think the asset gathering is more important. I once had a manager who said that if you can get the assets, the production will follow. I don't know if I will ever be as good as my father at managing money, but I would like to at least keep pace with the S&P.

You have got to take an active role in your clients' lives nowadays, because there are a lot of things that change. If you don't keep up with those, you are really not doing your job as a financial planner. We also build relationships with our clients' children, because ultimately they are going to have the assets, and they want to trust the person who is managing it.

ANGELOTTI: I think we are in a changing business now. Transactional brokerage is on the way out, with E-Trades and discount brokerage giving people the ability to make trades on their own computers. If you can't offer value-added services, you are going to die in this business. We are experts in financial planning, estate planning, and asset management.

When I came into this business with Northern Trust, our typical customers were in their mid-seventies, sometimes a widow, but certainly unsophisticated in terms of market nuances, and now that's totally different. With golden handcuffs, takeovers, and 401(k) accumulations, clients are retiring in their forties and fifties to Sarasota with a lot of assets and a great deal of sophistication. They watch CNBC every day; they are reading *Barron's* and *The Wall Street Journal.*

This partnership is what has made all the difference in our business. I can't imagine brokers not partnering in the future. If you're managing assets, you're not out gathering them, and vice versa. You need someone to bring in business, and you need someone to manage the business.

DORSEY: Tell me about your estate planning business.

ANGELOTTI: I was a tax attorney in Chicago and wrote a book on estate planning in 1979. When someone comes down to live in Sarasota, many times their first intuition is to hire an attorney to handle their estate. But if we can talk to them first about their estate, we usually get their business. Most CPAs understand their business very well, but most of them are not proactive with recommending ways to invest. If we can get a client and look at his whole portfolio, we are in a position to make recommendations. This allows us to get all of their business and not just a piece of it.

We frequently set up private foundations and work with clients on charitable remainder trusts and with replacement insurance trusts. If we are dealing with a client who looks like he has a beautiful portfolio and everything is established, we can still recommend some estate planning. We can set up a CRT, rearrange those assets, do a wealth replacement trust, or get a commission on the insurance.

DORSEY: Tell me what you think directly relates to your success.

E. ROSENBERG: As far as investments are concerned, we are in the midst of a demographic change, accompanied by a technological revolution. Years ago CDs were the biggest investment in a portfolio for the majority of Americans. Now they are able to access instant information through the computer and handle all their stock transactions on the computer. It's imperative for brokers to have a fee-based business, or risk being left out. If you don't have an approach that is a value-added approach to clients today, you will become unnecessary.

D. ROSENBERG: Part of our success, too, has been in being pro-active. We are not only proactive in stock selection, trying to find tomorrow's good stories, but I think we are proactive in keeping our customers informed on what is going on in the markets on a daily basis. When the market is down 500 points we're here all night calling them to explain what just happened.

> *". . . we are in the midst of a demographic change, accompanied by a technological revolution."*
>
> ED ROSENBERG

DORSEY: How do you charge for your services?

E. ROSENBERG: We charge our clients 2 percent on a wrap basis, so we discount somewhat from the top fee allowable. We do have some commission business, but we are trying to get all of our clients on a fee-based arrangement.

DORSEY: And then at the 2 percent level, they don't pay commission on that, is that right?

E. ROSENBERG: No, it's a wrap. Our goal is to have every client under some form of management by the year 2000. We want to get to a point at which the only transactions we enter into are on behalf of managed clients. We combine top-notch fundamental research with Point and Figure technical analysis. We also add a few stocks of our own that we do research on. We are always in tune with what's going on in the market and just about everything we need to know about the stocks we own or want to own.

DORSEY: Explain that to me. Once you have a position, how do you manage it? What do you do when things go wrong?

E. ROSENBERG: When things go right, we just stay with that position. If the fundamentals are negative, and the technicals still remain positive, we would hold on.

DORSEY: When selecting a fundamentally sound stock from one of your resources, do you take the relative position of the sector into consideration?

E. ROSENBERG: Yes. If the stock was right and the sector was high, we would be reluctant to buy it. There are many cases in which we would sell a stock that's still on a highlighted list or sell out of a sector before it comes off a highlighted list. I chart forty-one sectors a week, and if we think a sector is breaking down, we are more inclined to get out of it than we would if the sector's influence is great.

DORSEY: Does one of you manage the public relations? It seems that every time I turn around I see you mentioned in a magazine or in the *Sarasota Times*. It's absolutely amazing the type of write-ups that you gentlemen have gotten in the past.

D. ROSENBERG: We don't have a PR person. It's just been something that we have been fortunate with. We have been in the right place at the right time with the right profile, and consequentially, we do get a lot of press. It's comforting to our clients and also appealing to new prospects. Our PR staff tends to consist of our thousand or so clients who constantly refer new people to us every single day. Those are the best PR people to have.

DORSEY: It sounds as though with the three of you, all bases are covered in your business.

DICK ANGELOTTI is Senior Vice President of investments at Morgan Keegan & Co. in Sarasota, Florida. Before teaming up with Ed and David Rosenberg, he was a practicing attorney in Chicago for thirteen years specializing in estate planning and tax practice. He went on to work for Northern Trust Bank, Bank of Boston, and PaineWebber.

EDWARD ROSENBERG graduated from the State University of New York and earned his MBA in Finance and Economics from Pace University. His professional background includes positions as a portfolio manager at Barnett Bank (formerly United First Federal) and President of Southern Florida Bank.

As the youngest member of the Angelotti/Rosenberg group, DAVID ROSENBERG has already established himself in the investment world. After graduating from the University of Notre Dame with honors, he worked as an investment executive for four years and collected numerous awards. Since 1994, he has worked for PaineWebber as a mutual fund coordinator and is now Associate Vice President for Morgan Keegan.

Nikki Chicotel and Sheila Burke
First Security Van Kasper
San Francisco, California

IF I WERE TO SUMMARIZE this partnership with one word it would be "service". Not only do Nikki and Sheila have a successful partnership, but they also have developed a specialty area dealing with customers in the technology field.

Nikki does all the research for the business, both fundamental and technical, and executes all the orders. Sheila is primarily involved in marketing and the other services they provide, like Rule 144 stock and options. They operate in San Francisco, so many of their clients are in the high-tech companies. They use specialists who understand the corporate stock option world. Sheila and Nikki get involved in every aspect of their client's financial life, from home mortgages to children's education funds. They get no remuneration for much of what they do for their clients. It's all part of the package when they become your adviser.

Building and maintaining their business has required long hours. There have been many occasions when my first call of the day came from Nikki at 6:30 A.M., which is 3:30 A.M. her time. When the trading session begins, she's prepared. Nikki and Sheila have great synergy in their partnership, which you will see in the following interview. Let's begin with Sheila Burke.

TOM DORSEY: Sheila, tell me about the beginning. When you did start the business and how did it all begin?

SHEILA BURKE: I started in the brokerage business in 1983. I was hired as a sales assistant to one of the founding partners at Van Kasper and Company in San Francisco. With a background in small business consulting, I enjoyed the broker/client relationship from the start. I was particularly fascinated by the excitement and challenge. Remember, there was no bull market back then! In fact, investors would laugh at me when I tried to tell them about the benefits of buying stocks. At that time, money market rates were paying 11 to 12 percent! It was a tough sell, but one that would prove to be lucrative later.

Van Kasper & Company was young and growing, and it was great to be in on the ground floor of that growth. Some of the great technology and biotech companies were going public then. So it was an exciting time in the business.

After a year of sales assistant training, I was ready to take the plunge to become a broker. I am grateful to the management of Van Kasper for giving me an opportunity to prove myself. They agreed to sponsor me as a broker, and the rest is history. But by 1990, I was burned out from the twelve-hour days of prospecting and building my business. I needed a sabbatical, so I took a two-month leave of absence. Shortly after my return, I had a conversation with Steve Adams, one of the firm's founders. He suggested I consider teaming up with Nikki because we had different but complementary areas of interest and expertise. At that time, Nikki was a branch manager at another Van Kasper office. The idea appealed to both of us, and out of that conversation we formed a partnership that is now in its eighth year.

NIKKI CHICOTEL: After the crash of 1987, Sheila and I published a newsletter with Steve Adams, a Van Kasper managing partner. We started working more closely together after that. We would share stock, marketing, and prospecting ideas. I was already computerizing my stock selection database, and Sheila started a library of marketing and prospecting campaigns on her computer. That's how the partnership first started. We pooled our respective specialties.

When Sheila took her sabbatical, I managed her clients for about two months. It produced an instant increase in the assets that we track. Her clients were enjoyable, and Sheila left good records. When she returned in the fall of 1990 to find her business intact, we started talking about partnership.

I think our partnership has grown stronger and more productive over the years, which ultimately benefits our clients.

BURKE: As our confidence in each other grew over the years, we found it most productive for each of us to focus on our areas of expertise. Nikki loves to research companies and is excellent at analytical work. I am at my best interacting with clients, reviewing their investment goals, determining the best methods of implementation, and developing new clients.

We continually bounce ideas off each other, whether it's determining stock strategy in a down market or how to develop a stock option strategy for a new client. We firmly believe our clients are getting the best of both worlds.

DORSEY: Nikki, I understand you were a branch manager at one time. Tell me about it.

CHICOTEL: I got my start in 1968 working in the mailroom at Merrill Lynch. That was supposed to be my temporary job until I went to college, but I got so excited about the stock market that I just stayed in the business. When I was old enough to qualify, I got my broker's license. I worked with a broker partnership for a few years. I saw even back then how a partnership could operate successfully. I ended up working at a firm called Bateman Eichler.

DORSEY: You have quite a bit of experience at this point with lots of years left before retirement.

CHICOTEL: Yes, nearly 30 years of experience. I've operated through all kinds of markets. When I left Bateman Eichler, I went to Shuman Agnew. Then I went to the buy side for a while. I traded stocks at Fields, Grant and Company, a money management firm. I learned about trading stocks, covered option writing, and portfolio management. Fields, Grant was one of the first money managers to computerize. They punched cards, and bought time on Stanford University's computer to process the client reports. That was cutting-edge technology at the time. I returned to the "sell" side in 1976 with the advent of discounted commissions. C. D. Anderson and Company hired me to manage their compliance and organize their office. Our only competition was Charles

Schwab. Eventually Security Pacific Bank bought the company. In 1982, Van Kasper hired me to open a new branch office in Marin County, California. A year or two later, I abandoned the security of a salary to be a full-time broker.

DORSEY: Sheila, tell me the difference between operating as an individual broker and working within the partnership that you and Nikki now have. What are the differences, the good points, and the bad points?

BURKE: The good points far outweigh the bad. Particularly, over time, we have both seen the benefits to operating as a "team." Both Nikki and I firmly believe that the broker of the new millennium must take a consulting approach with clients to survive. So we are an idea whose time has come.

"Nikki loves to research companies. . . .

I am at my best interacting with clients. . . .

We firmly believe our clients are getting

the best of both worlds. "

SHEILA BURKE

That's not to say that adjustments didn't have to be made. Both of us were very independent and "take charge" people. We each had to learn to defer to the other partner in her area of expertise. For example, when Nikki completes an analysis of a particular stock, we will both review the information together. And then we will jointly agree on the final decision to buy or not to buy. When we make a proposal to a client on stock option strategy, I'll do the background research and then review it with Nikki for her input before presenting it to the client.

CHICOTEL: We play devil's advocate for each other's area, but almost never disagree. We have built up trust over the years.

DORSEY: What is your minimum account size?

CHICOTEL: $150,000.

DORSEY: So, if a person came to you with under $150,000, he wouldn't get the benefit of your services?

CHICOTEL: No, because he would be overpaying for our services. A beginning investor is best serviced by investing in mutual funds. We're willing to direct them to a mutual fund group we like. When their assets get to the point where they can invest $150,000, they usually need the rest of our services. I will say that we have a goal for next year in our business plan to train our licensed sales assistant to be able to manage smaller accounts.

There are strategies and programs that we would enjoy doing with smaller accounts if we had the personnel. Specific programs include the Dow Relative Strength Five and the Sector Five programs. I chart all of those components, but we just do not have the time and energy to provide the education.

DORSEY: Nikki, tell me exactly how you operate your side of the partnership.

CHICOTEL: All client accounts are entered on the computer. We specify what percentages of the assets should be in stocks, bonds, and cash; whether it's an aggressive or conservative account; and whether or not they are qualified to trade options. The account information is in the computer, the money is in the account, the asset mix agreed upon, and it's time to invest. I create my buy list based on fundamental analysis and technical analysis, using several sources of research like *Value Line,* S&P, Van Kasper, and other respected firms on the street. And I use Dorsey, Wright's technical service to help with timing and to narrow the field to a manageable batch of securities. We use the NYSE bullish percent as our guide to determine whether we will be aggressive or defensive.

There is a strict checklist I use for every stock. I start with the general market risk and then the individual sector risk. We use the sector bullish percents to determine when it's a good time to initiate a position. When the market risk is very high, we often use covered call writing. When we are ahead 25 to 30 percent on a stock, I'll usually sell one-third to one-half of it. When the stock is up 50 percent, I usually sell another third. We will hold on to the last part of the position until the price breaks the long-term bullish support line, which could be days, weeks, or years.

In the last year, the market moved up so quickly we were "forced" by this discipline to take a lot of profits. This year, when the NYSE bullish percent reversed down, we had higher than usual cash positions and were able to avoid a lot of the decline that followed. When the various sectors begin to rotate back up, we will find stocks that are attractive at the same time we have cash. This strategy encourages us to do exactly what we ought to be doing in the market. When things become overheated, we are selling and taking profits, and when the market pulls back, we will have cash to reinvest.

DORSEY: So you still subscribe to that old school of thought, buy low and try to sell high? It's a philosophy that is not favored on Wall Street these days.

CHICOTEL: Yes. I do not bottom fish. We are not that aggressive. We don't try to catch a falling knife.

DORSEY: When do you write covered calls?

CHICOTEL: When the NYSE Bullish percent reverses down from above 70 percent, we like to mitigate the downside risk by writing calls on our long positions. I have a worksheet that lets me determine how much we will profit if our stock is called, and how much downside protection we will have if the stock declines. First and foremost, the stock must meet our fundamental and technical criteria. Sometimes when a stock is just a little higher than I would like to pay, writing a call brings it down to my buy price. That premium coming in makes it worth buying. So when the risk/reward is not good enough on the stock itself, I adjust it by selling a call, which in effect reduces the entry price.

DORSEY: But you normally won't write covered calls until you feel that the market is at a relatively high level?

CHICOTEL: That is right, or if it looks as though it's just going to be flat for a time, that's another way to generate positive returns. You don't want any dead assets.

DORSEY: So if the market was perceived as low, such as when the NYSE Bullish Percent is in the 30 percent area, then you would not be writing calls against any stocks?

BURKE: Typically not. When the NYSE Bullish Percent is low and moving higher, we prefer to just buy a stock outright. When the NYSE Bullish Percent is high, but headed south, then we will write covered calls. Sometimes I will buy put options, too, if the market looks risky.

DORSEY: You will do that in some accounts because the risk is defined?

BURKE: In some qualified accounts, but not very many. We'll buy calls as a stock substitute and put the cash we would normally invest in a stock into the money market fund. And we never overleverage.

The other area in which we write calls is when clients have concentrated positions in their company stock. Most of our clients are in Silicon Valley, and a large portion of their net worth is tied up in stock options. They have the difficult decision of either exercising their options and incurring a large tax bite, or holding them with the downside and expiration risk. We develop a plan for them to exit their stock in an orderly fashion. It is designed both to potentially reduce taxes and to provide a strategy that they can stick with through the market ups and downs. We generally recommend clients set a goal of 10 to 20 percent of their overall financial assets invested in their company stock. If they leave their company, we will also use our program of writing covered calls to reduce their concentrated position.

DORSEY: So they are perfectly willing to let this stock go if they are called away?

CHICOTEL: They need to be, but, of course, sometimes if the stock continues up, they aren't thrilled, but they still have many more shares benefiting from the rise.

DORSEY: But they understand all possible scenarios before the trade goes on?

CHICOTEL: Yes.

DORSEY: Do you do anything with Rule 144 stock?

BURKE: I am the expert on Rule 144 stock. We do a regular business in restricted stock. Here again, we recommend that clients develop a strategy to reduce their concentrated position over time.

DORSEY: Dealing with restricted stock can be a challenge. Restricted stock must be everywhere in Silicon Valley.

BURKE: It is, Tom. One of the decisions we made when we started out together as partners was to focus on a specific client base. We wanted to become experts so that we actually knew more about their problems than they did. That was our mantra.

DORSEY: And how do you accomplish that mission?

BURKE: To do that effectively, we have to know all their life issues and financial concerns. From the beginning, our client base has been individuals in high technology businesses and secondarily, the retail business sector. These individuals' net worth has been primarily developed through stock options. So, of course, their primary concern is how best to manage this asset. In the Bay Area, wealth is determined by the value of their stock options, not salary. For example, if a client works at a private company that's going public, they want advice on when and how much of their stock to sell. Given the many restrictions on Rule 144 sales, that is a challenge. They also want to know Wall Street's view of the stock once it is public. We guide them through the entire process of determining how and when to sell restricted stock, monitoring the stock once it is public, and developing a strategy to reposition the proceeds from the sale.

> *"One of the decisions we made when we started out together as partners was to focus on a specific client base. We wanted to become experts so that we actually knew more about their problems than they did. That was our mantra."*
>
> SHEILA BURKE

DORSEY: Tell me what you do to effect a 144 (restricted stock) sale.

BURKE: First, we strategize with the client to determine how much stock to sell. Then we determine what kind of restricted sale it is. The client completes the appropriate paperwork and we follow it through the various compliance and legal departments to get the final approval for sale. If it is a difficult stock to trade, we work closely with the trader to effect an exit that will cause the least disruption in the trading pattern of the stock.

DORSEY: How do you handle stock option exercises?

BURKE: Again, we first discuss strategy with the client and determine how much stock to sell. Then the client completes the proper paperwork and we follow it through the legal departments until we get the OK to sell. This particular transaction is called a "cashless option" trade because the client puts up no capital to do the transaction and we, the brokerage firm, handle the entire process, including sending the company a check for the cost basis and taxes.

DORSEY: Give me a typical case, Sheila. Let's say I work at Sun Microsystems, and I have thousands of Sun stock options. I am concerned that my assets are way overconcentrated in this stock but historically, the stock has been a good performer. I also have some options that are close to expiring, and I trade as an insider. What should I do?

BURKE: First of all, I would ask for a copy of your company stock option summary sheet. This document lists your grant date, exercise price, number of shares vested, and number of shares already sold. I will want to know the expiration date for your options since stock options do eventually expire if not exercised. I want to know whether you plan to stay at the company or envision leaving within the next few years. I would also want to know whether the options are non-qualified or incentive stock options, because the tax treatment differs.

DORSEY: What's next?

BURKE: Once we review all this information, we can make a recommendation. We recommend that clients sell a certain percentage of their options annually to avoid the risk of overconcentration. Clients tend to stay overconcentrated in their company stock because so many companies in Silicon Valley have done well. It is hard to argue with success. On the other hand, the Valley is replete with disasters that don't get much publicity. Sound money management principles dictate some asset allocation policy, so we continue to recommend an orderly diversification strategy.

Clients do worry because they don't want to be caught in a situation in which their stock drops dramatically as just happened to Computer Associates and other tech stocks in the recent market correction.

A cashless option trade is complete when the funds are wired to the company and the stock is delivered to us. I generally get a copy from the company of the "Confirmation of Sale" that itemizes the components of the trade. Some of this information is helpful because we also withhold extra taxes that the company didn't withhold in a money market account but that will be due. If we retain part of the stock, meaning all wasn't sold at the exercise, then we enter a new date and cost going forward for tax purposes.

> *"We consider ourselves the financial caretakers of our clients' lives, and our goal is to assist them in creating financial wealth and balance."*
>
> NIKKI CHICOTEL

DORSEY: This sounds like quite a lot of work. Are there any fees involved that you charge these people for this type of service?

BURKE: Most of our accounts are managed accounts, so we do not charge a commission. Rather, we charge a fee based on a percentage of assets under management. Therefore, this entire process is just part of our service. There are no extra fees involved. The trade itself can be done for $10 under our Managed Fee Program, a significant savings to the client instead of paying commissions. Our entire program of value-added services includes stock option strategies, portfolio management, retirement planning including

401(k)s, personal budgetary planning, repositioning inheritance portfolios, and children's education planning.

DORSEY: This sounds like a lot of extra work that one would normally do above and beyond trade execution.

CHICOTEL: Our clients consider us their financial consultants, and that's how they introduce us. We are not introduced as stockbrokers or money managers. They tend to consult with us on all their finances. We are basically fee-based brokers with a financial management component. If an issue concerns their finances, then we need to be involved. In the long run, these issues affect their personal finances, and our job is to manage their personal finances. To best do our job we need to be involved in all aspects of their finances. We currently advise a number of clients on how to assist their elderly parents in their finances. We consider ourselves the financial caretakers of our clients' lives, and our goal is to assist them in creating financial wealth and balance.

BURKE: The reason we offer such "valued-added" services is because as I listen to clients, their primary issues are time and how best to allocate their resources. They have a need for this kind of comprehensive advice. Clients are extremely demanding these days. Competition for their money is intense. Our clients are extremely intelligent, and not in the least intimidated by investments or trading on the Internet. They invented the technology surrounding it! They need more from us than just money management. They expect good performance and want to know that we are on top of it. They want to know what the market is doing and why. And they want specific, thoughtful advice about their particular issues. A mutual fund cannot deliver that kind of service.

CHICOTEL: We also review the financial profile of any public company the client is considering as a prospective employer.

DORSEY: Can you expand on that?

CHICOTEL: I just talked to a client who is considering moving from a very large firm to a startup, so there are a lot of things to consider. Sheila, why don't you talk about the two stocks we studied for a client to help him decide?

BURKE: Because our client base is in such high demand, they frequently receive multiple job offers. Even though they may know the company through its products or have friends working there, they still want an unbiased analysis of the company from a financial and investment standpoint. They don't have easy access to that kind of data. They are also concerned about leaving potentially millions of dollars' worth of stock options on the table.

There are difficult risks associated with working at a company with high turnover versus a stable company. They want to be sure to consider all the issues before making a career change. So, we will talk about how much they are leaving on the table in stock options and how that affects what they ask for in a new compensation package.

If the company is public, Nikki will also do an analysis of the stock, reviewing it from a fundamental and technical perspective. It is important to view the company from a risk/reward standpoint.

CHICOTEL: We check whether or not the credit reporting agencies have upgraded them or downgraded them recently. That is their salary at risk, too. We check the debt rating on the company.

BURKE: We also tell clients when we believe they are in companies that are suffering financially. We will tell them when they have too much of their own money tied up in the company, an added degree of risk that affects their financial picture.

CHICOTEL: Whether they take the advice or not doesn't matter. Clients are not going to resign just because we tell them that their company looks as if it is in trouble. But they will remember that we told them that they were at risk, and that we have nothing to gain or lose by that. There is no fee attached to that kind of advice and that kind of genuine concern and interest.

DORSEY: Sheila, you get involved in your clients' children's finances early on. Tell me about that.

BURKE: Many of our clients have children, and we encourage them to start a custodial account for the child as soon as they can. The earlier in a child's life that a parent sets up a custodial account, the less painful it is for the parent later. Depending upon how much and how early they fund a child's account, we recommend stocks, bonds, or mutual funds. Once a year, we run a children's education software program to see if we are on track with the funds that will be needed for their education. We then make adjustments annually, usually in January.

> *"Having this partnership is what allows us to offer a higher standard of service."*
>
> SHEILA BURKE

BURKE: In January we also remind clients to make their annual IRA contributions. We have standard letters of authorization, and we automatically transfer funds from their personal accounts into their IRAs or children's accounts. It's another value-added service we do so they don't have to think about it, and they know that their kids are taken care of. It's one less problem to deal with in life.

DORSEY: You mentioned to me earlier, Sheila, that you and Nikki used to meet annually to set business goals. Tell me about that.

BURKE: When we first began collaborating, we would meet in January to set our business goals. We would also include personal and educational goals. Topics we cover include how to increase productivity, new productivity tools, revenue growth, direction of the market, new investment tools, new services for clients, improving service, staffing, and impediments to our goals.

Business is changing so dramatically, we need to meet quarterly to reassess our strategies and goals. New technologies, client needs and concerns, and the furious pace of the bull market have all dictated a "real-time" response. Sometimes with clients we see reasons to meet earlier than the usual annual meeting—particularly in cases where clients are transitioning to a new job. In their first year, I often meet with new clients every three months, some of them every six months, so they understand our program.

We use a combination of fundamental and technical analysis. Many investors are not familiar with technical analysis, so we want to be sure to add education to our Client Review list when I meet with them. We also want them to understand our criteria for buying and selling stocks. I will bring technical charts of specific companies to client meetings so they can get a picture of something that is difficult to explain verbally.

We want our clients to know that we have a plan, we know how to execute it, and we will execute it. All active clients are scheduled to be called at least every two months. And we send and receive e-mails on a daily basis. In this way, we can become and stay part of their daily landscape.

DORSEY: I think that most people are not willing to go that extra mile.

CHICOTEL: It's a lot of work. I arrive in the office at 5:00 A.M. and work until the market closes at 1:00 P.M. I put in a good sixty hours a week, but it's sixty hours of doing things that I love. I enjoy contact with our clients. They call me to discuss specific stocks and strategies, so I don't miss them completely. Sheila and I are now each doing what we do best. That's another benefit of the partnership: the client pays one fee for the expertise of two experienced people.

BURKE: I believe that the competition is so fierce that you must have a program to present to clients, and you must know and believe in it and have a way to execute it. Then you must be able to convey that program to clients. Even then, there is no guarantee a client won't be upset because we sold a stock that then turned around and went back up, or that they didn't match the S&P 500 their first year of investing with us. So we have to really believe in the quality of the service we offer to clients. Having this partnership is what allows us to offer a higher standard of service.

SHEILA F. BURKE is a Senior Vice President of First Security Van Kasper in San Francisco. She came to Van Kasper in 1983 from a background in small business consulting. Sheila is a graduate of the University of Maryland, a member of Women in Technology International, and an associate member of the Institute of Electrical and Electronics Engineers, Inc.

NIKKI CHICOTEL also is a Senior Vice President at First Security Van Kasper in San Francisco. She began her career in 1968 and has worked in various sectors of the finance industry including compliance, trading, and portfolio management. She is involved in community affairs and serves on the Salvation Army Services to Seniors Council.

USING TECHNICAL ANALYSIS

THE TERM *technical analysis* conjures up varied mental pictures in minds of investors. Some view it as black magic, hocus pocus, high mathematics, or sophisticated analysis understood only by professionals. And yet others see it as a simple tool to record the imbalances between supply and demand. Those who don't really understand technical analysis dismiss or berate the concept, while those who take the time to become craftsmen in it can more effectively manage their clients' portfolios.

When I first entered the business, technical analysis was a lost art. Fundamental analysis had taken the driver's seat with the writings of the late great Edwards & Magee. The only person I knew who looked at charts back then was a rookie broker who started in the business about the same time I did. His name was Guy Miller. He always had a reference book of charts on his desk that he reviewed prior to any stock purchase. I don't know if they helped him or not, but he was the only broker I saw using them. There was no place for technical analysis where I worked, Merrill Lynch, Pierce, Fenner & Smith. As far as we were concerned, we didn't need anything more than specific direction from Merrill's home office. When they recommended buying a stock, we did. But stock analysis is not an either/or proposition. One method of analysis is not necessarily better than another, but I've found that the best results are achieved when one melds both schools of thought to accomplish one goal—that of making your client more money with less risk. The "less risk" part of that sentence is a very important consideration.

"I believe the best investment results are

obtained when both technical and

fundamental analysis are used together."

THOMAS DORSEY

I think that many technical methods are too complicated and subjective for the majority of investors to learn. There are dozens of technical strategies including Fibbonocci Retracement numbers, Gann Angles, waves and cycles, bar charts, candlestick charts, line graphs, quantitative analysis, neural networks, moving averages, Bollinger Bands, MACDs, relative strength index calculations, Point and Figure charts, and even astrology. As anyone who knows my work will tell you, I am a disciple of Point and Figure charting.

In fact, I've spent much of my career teaching this method to other brokers. No book written by me would be complete without strong emphasis on this method.

I favor Point and Figure analysis because of its simplicity and foundation in basic economic supply and demand theory. Since I believe the best investment results are obtained when both technical and fundamental analysis are used together, I have interviewed two brokers for this chapter who have used both methods expertly to develop and manage their business. I strongly recommend that you take a close look at these strategies.

To learn more about the Point and Figure method that is discussed in this chapter, see "The Basics of Point and Figure Charting," on page 234. Then, after you're ready for more in-depth lessons, pick up my book *Point and Figure Charting* (Wiley Finance Edition, 1995. $59.95).

INTERVIEW

Craig M. Wiener, PaineWebber Incorporated
Memphis, Tennessee

CRAIG WIENER IS A BROKER with PaineWebber in Memphis, Tennessee. I have known Craig for a number of years and have watched as his business has developed. I have had Craig speak at our Stockbroker Institutes in the past on the topic of prospecting. I've seen Craig's confidence rise significantly over the years as he has come to believe that combining his knowledge of Point and Figure technical analysis with his firm's great fundamental research has yielded exceptional results. Craig's business is centered primarily on equity management, which has helped him to build a business in excess of a million dollars a year in production. But let me stress that the high numbers aren't the most important part of Craig's story. Craig is one of those brokers who truly has his clients' interests at heart.

TOM DORSEY: Craig, give me a little background on how you first got into the business.

CRAIG WIENER: Well, I ended up going to Houston in 1985 right out of school to work for a penny stock firm. I worked there for about a year and a half until I realized I could do a better job for my clients by accepting a position at Morgan Keegan in my hometown of Memphis. They gave me an open door to join the firm when I was ready.

DORSEY: Once you got to Morgan Keegan how did you begin to develop your business?

WIENER: Well, at first I operated pretty much like all the other brokers at the firm. I read the market analysis and stock recommendations on our focus list put out by research, as most brokers do. I called my clients, told them what stocks were on the focus list, and we bought them when they were put on the list and sold them when they were taken off. Plain vanilla.

"I took a chance and sold the stock, every single share, in one day—100,000 shares. I felt sick to my stomach doing it. . ."

CRAIG WIENER

DORSEY: Did you make calls to generate business?

WIENER: I didn't like to cold call. The way I got around cold calling was to develop a weekly newsletter to get my name out in front of high-net-worth prospects. The newsletter helped these prospects get to know me before I called them. It briefed them on certain stocks I thought they should consider—and as the calls started coming in I became more comfortable calling these prospects back with other recommendations. That's how I built my business. My business increased at a fairly steady rate for a few years until 1994. In 1994 it seemed that it didn't matter what anybody was recommending, everything just went down. At that time Eileen Phelan, a department manager at Morgan Keegan, had been recommending the use of Point and Figure charting for a couple of years. She had learned it from you and your group.

DORSEY: As a matter of fact, Morgan Keegan was one of our very first customers when we went into business in 1987.

WIENER: Although this was not official firm opinion, Eileen Phelan had been urging us to avoid certain stocks all through 1994. We had been doing so well for so long that most brokers just ignored her. But her picks were right on. Well, I started paying attention to technical analysis after that. In late 1994, heartbroken with my stock picks, I learned how the Point and Figure method of analysis worked. That's when the light came on. I was very apprehensive at first. In fact, when everybody was saying the bull market is over and the world is coming to an end, I was stunned by the fact that the technical indicators were in fact saying that it was as good a buying opportunity as we had seen in a while. I sat back and just watched for the first couple of months in 1995, and I was stunned by the fact that we were actually in the beginning of the next leg up in the great bull market, or what looked like it was. It was at that time I became confident with the indicators. I started religiously watching them at this point and incorporating them into my business. I watched the sectors rotate as the Bullish Percent Indicators suggested, and step by step started to apply the Point and Figure analysis to our fundamental work at Morgan Keegan. My equity performance improved dramatically.

DORSEY: When did you realize that technical analysis was really working for you?

WIENER: The year 1995 was a defining moment for me. A stock that was widely recommended as the next great winner in the market caught the attention of many brokers. I was a little slow to buy it. I was apprehensive to buy it on fundamentals alone. When it became technically sound, I decided to buy it, and I bought a lot of it. The stock did not go up but instead broke down technically, and this was really a defining moment. The fundamentals were still strong and the stock was still being recommended. I decided that if I was to have faith in the Point and Figure method, I had to sell it. I decided overnight that I was going to go with my technical knowledge in this situation, which was totally against what the fundamentals suggested.

DORSEY: So you sold the stock against the firm's recommendation?

WIENER: Yes. I took a chance and sold the stock, every single share, in one day—100,000 shares. I felt sick to my stomach doing it, going against everything fundamental that told me to hold it. I sold it at $18. The vast majority of brokers held. The stock continued to break down. It just kept slipping into darkness. You can't imagine how good it feels to make such a gut-wrenching decision and have it be right, in spades. Although a decision like that will not always pan out this way, it did in this case. My contemporaries continued to buy the stock, and it never saw the light of day since then. To this day it still is not technically sound. It's trading at $3 to $4 of a point—a real business-killer.

DORSEY: So that's what did it for you? It changed your way of thinking from that time forward?

WIENER: Yes. This was the defining moment of my career. I operated contrary to popular belief in a big way and was right. Actually the charts were right, I just had the guts to follow them. I started incorporating Point and Figure analysis in my decision-making process from that point forward. I found the best way for me to operate in the equity markets was with fundamental and technical analysis. Probably more important than anything was that my confidence in my own abilities was extremely high. It's clear that the key to success for any broker is confidence.

DORSEY: Craig, did this new confidence have any affect on your production? It's great to be right, but did it translate into increased business for your firm and for yourself?

WIENER: My production went from about a quarter of a million in 1995 to about $750,000 by the end of 1996, and it has continually increased from there.

I should mention that I've recently moved to PaineWebber. I made the switch to PaineWebber because it focuses on the larger cap stocks I now deal with. Morgan Keegan is a great firm, but it follows the smaller cap issues, and my business was moving in the larger, more liquid, issues. So PaineWebber is the perfect place for me to operate my business.

> *"... This was the defining moment of my career. I operated contrary to popular belief in a big way and was right."*
>
> CRAIG WIENER

DORSEY: Would you suggest that most of that is a direct result of the increased confidence you have now, being able to apply both fundamental and technical analysis to your investment process?

WIENER: I would say that a lot of that was a result of being able to avoid disasters. I came to the realization that one of the keys to success in this business is to be able to keep my clients in the sectors that are technically sound. Nothing is perfect, but when you have a solid plan and work that plan, you tend to have more success. When to sell can be more important than when to buy. Many brokers never have a solid plan for what to do when things go wrong.

DORSEY: Craig, I know you have become very knowledgeable in this method. I've always been a real proponent of updating Point and Figure charts by hand. Even though you have our Internet database, you still do much of it by hand. How many do you update each day by hand, and what does this do for you?

WIENER: I've never counted them, but I think it's probably about 500 charts every day. What it does for me is very simple. It allows me to see sectors when they are moving off bottoms, or breaking out of tops. You begin to see tops when they begin rolling over. I told you a few days ago that when I first started doing technical analysis I used to look at these charts like everybody else did. I would look at the chart, and all I would see was Xs and Os up and down. Now when I look at charts, I really don't see Xs and Os. I see patterns, shakeouts, triangles, bear signal reversals, triple tops, bullish catapults, bearish catapults. The beauty of the Point and Figure method is there is no room for subjectivity. These charts totally take volatility out of the equation whereas bar charts leave volatility in. One must update a bar every day no matter how inconsequential the move is. You don't with a Point and Figure chart. That's why I can maintain so many charts each day by hand. It could never be done with bar charts. It's actually kind of funny, because when I try to teach this to clients or friends, it's hard for me to explain, because when I look at a chart I'm not looking at Xs and Os anymore. I see right through to the pattern.

DORSEY: The method is straightforward. There are no gray areas like you get with a bar chart. The bar chart is totally left up to subjectivity. Now, you go about this a little differently than most people, including myself. I look at the fundamentals first. I have a tendency to create an inventory of fundamentally sound stocks and then I go from there to the technicals. You have tendency to do it the other way around. Tell me how you go about selecting individual stocks.

WIENER: I will look at the technicals first, then when I find a great chart in a sector that is low and on offense, I will seek out the fundamental research. If the fundamental research does not support the technicals, it's a "no go." If I see a sector reversing up from an oversold level, it goes into bull alert (buy mode). I will use your Internet charting system and create a search for technically sound stocks that fit my parameters for the search. I then go to PaineWebber research to fit the fundamental side of the equation to the stock I have deemed technically fit. I will see whether PaineWebber follows the stock, I will check out the fundamental research on the company, and I'll go from there.

> ## *"The beauty of the Point and Figure method is there is no room for subjectivity."*
>
> ### C R A I G   W I E N E R

DORSEY: So the chart is the first thing that catches your eye. Because you are updating so many charts by hand every day, you will naturally see a great number of potential buy candidates. It's interesting how each broker uses the same information a little differently. I like to go to lists like *Value Line* rank 1, for instance, and then filter for the right technical picture. I use many fundamental lists. I just feel more comfortable knowing the lists I use are deemed fundamentally fit by some authority in that school of thought before I embark on my search for the technical fit. Either way leads to the same conclusion.

WIENER: Tom, I trust myself now with my abilities to apply the technical approach to my equity business. I trust myself first, which is why I look at the charts first, and then I move to the fundamentals. For the fundamental research I pretty much have to rely on other people who are specialists in that field. I'm considered the specialist in the technical side, so I feel more comfortable coming from that angle. I work as a team with my fundamental research department, and so far it's been magical.

DORSEY: Now, I heard you mention the term *sector.* How do you look at the overall market and then the sectors within the market? Do you use a bottom-up approach or top-down approach?

WIENER: I take the top-down approach. The first thing I'll do is look at the New York Stock Exchange and the Over-The-Counter Bullish Percent Indexes. These indicators calculate the percentage of stocks underlying the index which are on Point and Figure buy signals. High readings above 70 percent suggest that most investors have already visited the market and are fully invested. Low readings below 30 percent suggest the opposite: that most market participants have sold, and the availability of supply to force the market lower is limited. I try to confine my stock purchases to sectors that are on the low side, as I mentioned above.

> *"To help stay focused, I put signs directly in front of me. The most important sign in my office is 'Buy on pullbacks.'"*
>
> CRAIG WIENER

DORSEY: So, in a nutshell, you look at the overall market, offense or defense. If offense, you look for a sector that is low and on offense. Then you search that sector for technically sound stocks, and you fit the fundamentals to the stocks in that inventory. Finally, if and when everything matches up in a particular stock, you build a position. Having the confidence to build a big position must result in bigger production.

WIENER: That's how my production has increased so significantly. Your recap is exactly what I do. It's a perfect example of a day in my life, or it's really more like a week in my life. The business is so much fun when you have a logical, organized plan of attack and the confidence to work that plan.

DORSEY: Even if you only maintain fifteen stocks a day, it's going to boost your confidence by helping you better understanding the overall market. How do you organize this thought process? I know you use a system to keep track of the breakouts.

WIENER: It's impossible for me to retain all the breaks and patterns in my mind. In order to retain the actual breaks and patterns, I've devised a grid on a piece of paper that I have in front of me. As I'm charting on this grid I have a section for strong buy, and a section for buy. Stocks that go on the strong buy side are stocks in my book of charts that are in sectors below 50 percent. The buys are really the stocks in sectors that are above 50 percent but in bullish modes. The "buys" are in bullish modes but are not on strong buy because the sector is on the overbought side of the ledger. They shouldn't be considered as bullish as the strong buys. I put double checkmarks by each stock if the stock has actually pulled back to a strong support area. It gives my client an extraordinary risk/reward situation. The whole game, in my opinion, is risk versus reward. I try to take as little risk as possible when entering a position. The better the risk/reward, the higher the probability I will recommend the stock. So many brokers and investors never consider the risk/reward characteristics of any given position. This can be calculated easily by using the Point and Figure vertical and horizontal count of the potential move of the underlying stock. I always have a minimum of 2 to 1 and preferably better.

DORSEY: Craig, I was in your office a few weeks ago, and I noticed signs that you have in your office. They seem to be put up there to remind you of things. Could you cover a few of those for me?

WIENER: The signs are actually are very relevant today, with the bullish percent at 72 percent (considered high). To help stay focused, I put signs directly in front of me. The most important sign in my office is "Buy on pullbacks." At this point in the ballgame, if you are going to go long, the market with the Bullish Percent above 70 percent but still in a bullish mode, you should be thinking of recommending only stocks that are on pullbacks to support. Let's use XYZ Cheeseburger as an example. The stock was up to 56–57 the other day and it looked great, but when it pulled back to 51 it looked even better. When the market is at these lofty levels, you have got to be very, very patient. You may miss some, but there are a lot of trains out there leaving the station. I think you are better off waiting for them to pull back before you recommend them. Once again, we get back to risk versus reward. You are going to increase the risk/reward ratio for your clients if you have patience. So what if you miss a train or two? There are 12,000 stocks that trade out there.

DORSEY: In other words, buy stocks on sale?

WIENER: You have to buy stocks on sale.

DORSEY: In the XYZ Cheeseburger example that you just gave, waiting for the pullback could have saved you 10 percent. That can make a big difference in a portfolio over a year's time if you are able to capture a 10 percent advantage in every stock you buy.

WIENER: It can make a great difference in a portfolio over time, and it really makes a huge impression on new accounts, that you are working the buy or sell order. It seems that everyone is just interested in buying anything under the sun. They think stocks can't go down. I'm here to tell you they can and do. When you recommend to a new account to buy XYZ Cheeseburger at 51, and it's at 56, basically a 10 percent correction, they naturally don't think that's going to happen. But you really make an impression when the stock does pull back.

DORSEY: Craig, what advice would you give a broker that's just starting out today?

WIENER: I gave that advice about three years ago to a broker who asked me, "Is it going to be this difficult forever?" The advice I gave to him was to read your book, *Point and Figure Charting*. I told him to start maintaining his clients' charts each day and that sooner, rather than later, it would give him the ability to think more clearly about the investment process. We have a research and investment policy committee department to handle the fundamental work for us, and they do a great job here at PaineWebber. We can, however, take our technical expertise and combine it with our analysts' fundamental expertise and the results should be pretty good. It's allowed me to think on my own.

CRAIG WIENER is currently a financial adviser for PaineWebber in Memphis, Tennessee. He holds degrees from both the University of Tennessee and C. W. Post College. Before joining PaineWebber, Craig was a financial adviser at Morgan Keegan for ten years.

James A. Parrish, Jr., Morgan Keegan & Co., Inc. Nashville, Tennessee

JIM IS ONE OF the most solid brokers I know. He's gone through the ranks from broker to branch manager to regional director. Even though Jim is at the regional level of the business, he still maintains his large production while executing the duties of a regional director. Jim is an excellent Point and Figure technician. I am very proud to have been the one to bring this method to his attention. It has changed the way he does business, and the confidence with which he manages his accounts is at an all time high. If you want what he has, do what he does.

TOM DORSEY: Jim, you have developed a solid long-term business. You have worked your way up at Morgan Keegan to become an executive managing director. You don't get there by doing things halfway. Tell me about your early years in the business.

JIM PARRISH: After graduate school, I went to work for a bank as a loan officer in the commercial lending area, because I wanted to own my own business. I thought that the best way to do that would be to lend money to businesses so I would have access to their financials and figure out the best one to buy. I eventually bought an office equipment/furniture/computer business in Kentucky and was a 50 percent partner for five years. I had the option to buy the other 50 percent, but when they wouldn't sell I sold my half.

I had always wanted to be in the brokerage business, so I answered an ad in *The Wall Street Journal* for E. F. Hutton's fast-track management program. I joined Hutton in Nashville in 1985 and stayed as a broker and a trainer with the expectation of running my own office.

After the crash, Hutton was purchased by Shearson Lehman Brothers. I took a look at the brokerage business at that time and learned about Morgan Keegan. I had never really heard about the firm, so I visited Allen Morgan, the head of the company, and here we are. I was given the opportunity to open several Kentucky offices for Morgan Keegan, and now I'm branch manager of the Nashville office. I run a region that covers five states and about twelve offices.

DORSEY: How did you get started with Point and Figure charting?

PARRISH: In the beginning, I was like every other broker. I listened to the analysts, and wondered why stocks were going down when fundamentals looked good. When I was first introduced to Dorsey, Wright by one of your first customers, my understanding of the business began to change.

"I have been able to educate my clients using the example of playing a piano with two hands instead of just one: One hand represents the fundamental approach, and the other hand represents the technical approach. I use both methods together and that gives me the best results."

JIM PARRISH, JR.

At first, I learned just enough about what you do to be competitive. I started reading your daily report, and I became intrigued. One of the most important things I have done with the Point and Figure method of analysis is to maintain my own stock charts every day, and that has made a difference. Eventually I attended your Advanced Stockbroker Institute, and it's given me the ability to explain to clients why things happen in the equity markets. Most brokers never get a handle on why prices change in the market. But I have been able to educate my clients using the example of playing a piano with two hands instead of just one: One hand represents the fundamental approach, and the other hand represents the technical approach. I use both methods together and that gives me the best results. I've also brought my partners up to speed on this method. They are two young guys who are doing a great job, and they are out prospecting, so I've tried to make sure that we are all using the same methods.

DORSEY: How do you use technical analysis to prospect?

PARRISH: Morgan Keegan specializes in covering bank stocks, especially local banks. Making an initial presentation with a high-quality local bank is a good way to attract clients with large assets. So we chose the conservative way to become involved with an account. That is, owning a local bank stock leads us into a meeting to discuss their clients' other investment objectives. At the second meeting, we explain how technical analysis fits in with fundamental analysis and how these methods together explain why a particular stock has gone up or down.

Clients are really taken with the fact that they finally have a way to stack the odds in their favor. We are very careful to make them understand that this is not a fail-safe method. There is no perfect method of analysis. It is, however, the best we have seen and, in our opinion, must become a part of the investment process. Anyone who is willing to accept the law of supply and demand will usually accept the Point and Figure method of analysis.

Once we open the account, our next step is to explain our methodology to the client—fitting our fundamental research with Point and Figure technical analysis. We currently subscribe to First Boston for the big-cap research. We also have other outside services we subscribe to. We have put together two folders that explain how we fit both schools of thought together. One folder is for the client and one for us. We flip through it together, page by page, in about fifteen minutes. There is one picture in the presentation that makes a big impression, and it's the sector bell curve. If anyone understands anything about statistics, it hits home.

We have to do something to set ourselves apart from the sea of brokers who are out there trying to sell mutual funds and managed products. This is what makes us different. Don't get me wrong. We do raise money to be managed as well. Morgan Keegan has a very strong managed money program.

Once we have a client, we try to obtain all the financial information so we can do a total asset allocation plan. We create a written investment policy, which shows him how the assets are currently allocated, and some ideas on investments consistent with his risk tolerance and investment objectives. In almost every proposal, there is a recommendation for a small- or mid-cap manager for a portion of his assets. We offer ourselves as managers for that portion. We are not trying to go out and use our research and Point and Figure with the entire portfolio. We want it to be in the place where it fits the best.

DORSEY: If a client came to you with a half a million dollars of capital to invest and $200,000 which could be allocated to a small-cap manager, that is the portion you manage?

PARRISH: Yes. We will also offer them an alternative small-cap manager if they choose. Invariably they choose us for that portion of their portfolio. This is the added value that we bring to the table.

DORSEY: My days of prospecting would have been much easier if I had taken that plan of action. It makes so much sense, because many of these prospects are probably doing business with that local bank. They feel comfortable with it. The fundamentals in this case are what will probably create the sale. Then, this opens the door for us to explain exactly how we operate our business. I pretty much prospected with the next hot idea. The serious high-net-worth clients aren't interested in the next hot play. They are interested in building wealth, not gambling.

PARRISH: At Morgan Keegan, we train our brokers differently. We don't necessarily train brokers to gather assets. There is some merit to it, but we usually go against the grain. We have found that if you can just get a new client on the books rather than trying to go for all the assets the first time out, then more business will come. Once they become customers, the broker can take his time developing the relationship.

> *". . .all it will take is an extended bear market, which is out there somewhere, and these investors will find out how much guidance they really need. Brokers who have a solid plan for managing a client's money will be at a premium. "*
>
> JIM PARRISH, JR.

There are one or two ways to do that: One is to prospect with a tax-free bond, and I find that, quite frankly, boring. Another way is to find a bank that people can relate to. People are not intimidated by owning a bank stock, and that's been our best entree with a new client. We also prospect banks themselves, by calling on banks and finding out who does business with them. They are usually happy to give us lists of people to start sending information to. It's a win-win situation for the bank and for Morgan Keegan.

DORSEY: I'm willing to bet that the part you have managed has outperformed the other managers.

PARRISH: It's been interesting. Yes, we have beaten the benchmarks significantly. I think that our enthusiasm is contagious.

They can see in our eyes how excited we are about what we do rather than trying to be excited about what some manager in New York does.

DORSEY: You mentioned earlier that you update your charts by hand every day.

PARRISH: Yes, we update all of them by hand. I can't get a feel for it otherwise. Finally, my entire office understands the concepts of supply and demand and how it relates to the equity markets. We have a wrap program here at Morgan Keegan where a broker can operate on a discretionary basis, charge a wrap fee for managing an account. That's the way this business is going and we are working it in that direction, too. Soon we will be on a fee basis for managing equity money using Point and Figure and fundamentals.

DORSEY: Nowadays everyone offers the same services, whether you are Morgan Keegan or Merrill Lynch. Brokerage firms have become a commodity as has the information they dispense. Merrill Lynch has no advantage over you or Charles Schwab. The broker is going to become more responsible for the returns in his clients' accounts.

PARRISH: We have adopted that philosophy as a firm. When we open an account, we always send out the chart of the stock he just bought. They don't know what it is, and a lot of times they will call back and ask us to explain it, so we will start the process. This education process is so important, and it's just one more of those things that sets us apart from everybody else, because we will spend the time with them to fully explain the concept.

One of the reasons that I'm in this business is because it is intellectually challenging. It's a commitment, and there is no resting because the market doesn't rest. It's so great to have a way to navigate the ins and outs of the market. I never stop learning the little nuances that exist with Point and Figure method. It's one of the those things that, the more time you spend on it, the greater the gain.

DORSEY: Do you have any sell disciplines, Jim?

PARRISH: No, I don't do that. I used to try to use a 10 percent stop or so, and there is so much volatility in the market today that stops can happen very easily. There are clients who want to use stops, and when that is the case, we do it. But I try to discourage using stops because I can show so many cases, particularly in the technology sector, where they were stopped out of something that was up 30 percent in the next two months.

DORSEY: What if you are in a stock and the fundamentals clearly begin to change? Do you still stick with your original commitment?

PARRISH: When the fundamentals change but the chart still looks okay, I don't sell the stock. The analysts aren't always correct about the fundamentals.

DORSEY: Well, Jim, what do you see in the future for brokers? The Internet has made information a commodity. Discounters have made commissions a commodity. What's left for the full service brokerage firm?

PARRISH: When I retire, I want those $7 trades myself. I think after being in the stock market business for forty years, I'll be able to use this information and commissionless trading to my advantage. But individual investors who are trying to do it will find it difficult going it alone. We've had a great bull market and rising prices have bailed out those who otherwise don't have expertise. But all it will take is an extended bear market, which is out there somewhere, and these investors will find out how much guidance they really need. Brokers who have a solid plan for managing a client's money will be at a premium. Brokers who haven't got a clue will become order executors on a discount desk.

Most people who have a lot of money aren't trading on the Internet, because they don't have time to. One thing is for sure: there are fewer and fewer ways to provide value. The broker who can provide value will find more business. Knowledge will be at a premium.

DORSEY: We have got a two-sided situation. You have brokers who just come to work and they look on the shelf to see what's available, then they call somebody up and try to sell it. They send the firm's research out, and they do whatever everyone else does.

PARRISH: That broker is a dinosaur. I spend a lot of time recruiting brokers. When I find one who says that he looks at fundamentals and technicals together I nurture him. They'll do more business at Morgan Keegan, because I'll make sure it happens. It's something that I'm committed to, and I would like to see the whole firm committed to it some day. Wealth is built in the stock market and the better equipped a broker is to understand and manage his clients' funds, the more business he will do.

> As Executive Managing Director, JIM PARRISH functions in many capacities for the Nashville, Tennessee, office of Morgan Keegan. In addition to acting as a portfolio manager, he is also a regional manager covering four states and is a member of the company's eight-person Executive Committee. After graduating from the University of Kentucky, Jim worked as a commercial banker for five years, then went on to become president of an office equipment company and a broker for E. F. Hutton.

CHAPTER 9

THE MAKING OF A FINANCIAL MINISTRY

I'VE MET SO MANY fantastic brokers over the years, many of whom I deal with every day, so it was hard to pick out the one who stands at the head of the class. There are so many superb brokers, this book would never end if I included them all. Bob Woodall just kept coming to mind, because his strengths range across the spectrum.

He is one of the most accomplished equity managers I know. He has developed an amazing approach to technical analysis mixed with fundamental analysis. Bob would have also been a natural for the chapter on building relationships, because that is exactly what he has done so well over the years. Most brokers play to their strengths and capitalize on what they do best; Bob Woodall does a lot of things well. I think it's very worthwhile to explore his philosophy and strategy in greater detail.

INTERVIEW

Robert L. Woodall, Dain Rauscher
Dallas, Texas

TOM DORSEY: I would like you to take us through the early days when you first got into the market. What year was it?

BOB WOODALL: I first became a broker in 1966 after college and a string of unsatisfying jobs. I went to school to study theology and become a minister. But as I studied at Texas Christian University, my priorities changed. I realized that I wasn't really right for the ministry. I knew that I wanted to have some kind of pastoral presence in the world, but I felt that I was too materialistic to be a minister.

When I graduated in 1963 I was eligible for the draft so I signed up to go to Officers Candidate School (OCS) Naval School, in Newport, Rhode Island. But I ended up in the hospital with a severe back problem and needed to have my kidney removed. When I came out of the hospital in the latter part of 1963 I had to find a job, so I went to work as a manufacturing engineer for Texas Instruments. I did that for a couple of years but wasn't very happy.

Soon after that I ran into one of my TCU fraternity brothers who was working at Frances Du Pont in Dallas. Back in the '60s Du Pont, Bache, and Merrill Lynch were the three largest brokerage firms. He said that they were hiring trainees at Du Pont and, when I found out how much they were paying, I said I'd be there for the interview.

The brokerage business was very enticing to me from the very beginning because it's a place where you are rewarded for the amount of effort that you put into it. If you want to sit there and do nothing, you won't make money. If you want to get out and really make things happen, you can become very financially successful. I needed to get out of debt. I needed something that I could latch onto and feel motivated by. So that's how I got started.

> *"The brokerage business was very enticing to me from the very beginning because it's a place where you are rewarded for the amount of effort that you put into it."*
>
> ROBERT WOODALL

DORSEY: How did you develop your business in the beginning?

WOODALL: I came out of a standard wirehouse mentality. The early days of a broker's career is really what I call "dialing for dollars." You just sit there and dial the phone and try to talk anybody and everybody into getting involved with investments.

I left Du Pont in 1969 to start a brokerage company with several other gentlemen. We bought a small Midwest member firm, and we cleared through the Midwest Stock Exchange. In fact, the lady that we bought it from did primarily no-load funds. We got reciprocal soft dollars from them to do transactions on our seat in the Midwest Stock Exchange. We also began to develop our own clientele, and merged our firm into a New York Stock Exchange member firm in 1972.

DORSEY: And the market at that time?

WOODALL: In the late Sixties everything went up, just like today's bull market. The underwritings were great.

DORSEY: Were mutual funds big at that time?

WOODALL: Mutual funds were relatively small. We were beginning to see the start of Fidelity, and heard about some of the money managers coming out at that time, like Fred Carr and Gerald Seay. The mutual fund business had about fifty billion dollars in total assets. Today, Magellan alone has $16.7 billion in assets. An average daily volume was probably a million and a half to two million shares.

I will never forget the first day I saw ten million shares trade. We had an old translucent tape in our boardroom at the old Mercantile Bank that ran two hours late, with cellophane tape after the close. As a rookie, it was my job to change the tape, and I had blue ink from one ear to the other from changing that old cellophane tape. But ten million shares was a big day. Now we trade 600 million—amazing.

DORSEY: But the market climate changed.

WOODALL: In the market of '74 to '75, everything you touched would go down, day after day. I saw my production drop 80 percent. I was worried about supporting my wife and our twins—and I couldn't figure out how I was going to make a living other than learning to short the market. The only way you could stay in business in those days was shorting stocks.

DORSEY: Would customers be willing to sell short? Most customers today won't take that chance.

WOODALL: Back in those days, most people put their money into CDs or something long-term. But more active customers would trade in either direction.

DORSEY: How did you get started with technical analysis?

WOODALL: At first I bought a book on bar charts by John Magee and Robert Edwards called *Technical Analysis,* and I subscribed to Magee's charting service. I got his weekly letter, his charts, and his book. That's how I got into technical analysis. It really wasn't until the early '80s that I got into Point and Figure charts. There were very few services that you could buy good charts from then. There are so many different formations to figure out with bar charts that I finally thought that there had to be a better way. That's how I ran across some of the Chartcraft material and decided that I would begin to develop an understanding of what Point and Figure was. They were so much easier to maintain and to read.

DORSEY: Before that you were using fundamentals alone?

WOODALL: I got into technical analysis because I had done fundamental work for a long time. But as I continued to follow the fundamental side and the analysts' recommendation, I ended up getting bagged in stocks. And when my performance suffered, my business suffered, and when my business suffered my paycheck suffered.

I realized that I had to add another component to my stock market activity. I also needed to find reasonably good shorts, and you just couldn't find good shorts on the sell side of the brokerage business, because nobody ever recommended them. The only way to really find shorts was to do some technical work. That's how I ended up doing the Magee/Edwards thing and using that service.

Further on in my career, I began to realize that there were some good fundamental analysts and there were some bad ones. But I needed to take the good analysts and run those on an overlay with the technical counterpart. Seeing the technical picture with the fundamental picture gave me more personal confidence in my choices. In 1984 I moved to Dain Rauscher Pierce where I have remained since.

DORSEY: In 1974, when most people in the brokerage business lost most of their business, you were down to only 20 percent. How did you have the fortitude to stay afloat in the business when so many others were sinking?

WOODALL: I barely made it through. There was a piece of advice given to me by a gentleman who was a broker when I first started out in the business. He said, "I've been in the business a long time. This is a cyclical business. It has peaks and valleys, and some years you will make a lot of money and some years you can barely stay alive. The first piece of money that you get, save at least six months' worth of income and put it in a savings account where you can live off of it when the bad times come, because they will come."

That's exactly what I did. But when the market played itself out, I had eaten up six months' worth of income and was down to $800 in the bank. I went out on the front steps one night and wept because I did not know how I was going to make it through. I had one month's income left.

DORSEY: It sounds as if you were close to desperation.

WOODALL: I had such a defeatist outlook because business was so black, and it only got blacker. My attitude moved up and down with the Dow Jones Average. When you're on the upside, you're enthusiastic and positive, but when it's falling, you get down in the dumps. After eighteen months of this, my attitude and my self-worth just sort of fell apart.

At that point I realized that all I had left was prayer. So I asked for the Lord's help to change my attitude. I realized that if I changed my attitude, I could change my business—from transactions to relationships.

That was at the absolute bottom. But then the market turned up in 1975–76, and the business began to pick back up. That's when I really started developing and building this firm that I was in. We started doing some institutional work as the institutions became more active. I started doing some corporate finance and syndicate work, and we started adding brokers.

We got many of our clients invested in the oil and gas sector. My partner was a research analyst specializing in the area. We couldn't have picked a better time, coming out of the 1974–75 period, to be in oil and gas. And that's how the business took off. It wasn't anything specific that I did except hang on and plan for the future. It's been a wonderful business ever since.

DORSEY: How did you begin to meld business and the relationships in the way you managed accounts?

WOODALL: My career had some interesting turns. By 1982 we had built up a small regional firm here in Dallas, and we had a seat on the New York Stock Exchange. We did our own clearing, and we had an opportunity to sell the firm to a major wirehouse. I had gone to New York and negotiated a merger of the firm. I was not the largest shareholder in the company, so I could not force the deal. When I brought it back to my partners in Dallas, they decided that they didn't want to work for a major firm.

> *"I went out on the front steps one night and wept because I did not know how I was going to make it through. I had one month's income left."*
>
> R O B E R T   W O O D A L L

I thought that the oil and gas play was almost over. Since we had built our reputation on oil and gas, this was a good time to sell out at close to the top of the market. But my partners did not want to do that, so I decided to sell my stock and leave the firm to start another company. But I really missed the retail side. Retail was the ministry that I really wanted—the individual customers, rather than the institutional portfolio managers. Institutional customers look at the world differently than an individual investor does because they have their performance to worry about, and there's a lot of competition.

I became a branch manager at Dain Rauscher Pierce, but I didn't have much in the way of retail. By 1990, I was trying to rebuild a book for the third time. So I knew that this time, I was going to build my book on three basic fundamental premises:

safety, income, and liquidity. Those were the three basic cornerstones.

DORSEY: How did you plan to implement that?

WOODALL: First I decided to pick out a loss leader, so I chose U.S. Treasury bonds. I put together a yield curve that I carried with me. It had the U.S. Treasury yield curve compared with the triple-A municipal bond yield curve. Every time I spoke to a prospect, I would talk to them about Treasuries that I bought on the auction. I charged them the minimum amount of commission, and they absolutely loved it. Other brokers would not show them U.S. Treasuries because they made no money on it. And believe it or not, the more you can come in with safety and income and build a solid foundation of some fixed income in the portfolio, you began to see their stock business, and then you can begin to advise them on their equity positions. Every portfolio that I have has 25 to 40 percent in fixed income.

Asset allocation is a fundamental element to being a professional in this business. I might have some customers that don't want to have any fixed income, but they must know that there are good and bad times to be in the market. Those that are 100 percent equity should reduce that to 50 percent equities and 50 percent money market accounts.

DORSEY: Asset allocation is a buzzword that means many different things. Explain what you mean.

WOODALL: Asset allocation to me is made up of three components: cash and cash equivalents, fixed income, and equities. I have a percentage of each of those three items. Cash can be short-term Treasury bills or money markets. Fixed income can be municipal income, corporate bonds, or Treasuries. The equity side is primarily stocks.

It made a lot of sense to me to have some diversification in a portfolio that I could have some control over. After going through the REIT problem in the early '70s and through the utility problem with interest rates in the '80s, I realized that buying securities that pay dividends and get high yields was not the best thing to do. So I looked into buying fixed income. I thought that cash flow and bad markets were very positive for portfolios.

Some of the better portfolios that I have seen over the years had stocks that paid dividends or increased dividends. Cash is very important to a portfolio's overall value. My bonds are always laddered. That takes the guesswork out of managing a fixed-income portfolio. When a nearby bond matures, you go to the next ladder and slap on the next bond. It's almost like you are building an annuity for your business. I have bonds that come due every month that I replace on a ladder. The ladders can be out three years, five years, seven years, or ten years. I buy nothing but escrowed, guaranteed bonds with U.S. Treasuries sitting behind them. Individual customers, profit sharing plans, or 401(k)s always have fixed income. And I put them into Treasuries, agency papers, or high-grade corporate bonds when the time is right.

Fixed income adds a stability factor to portfolios so that in bad times, you're getting some positive results to offset the negatives in equity. The equity positions change based upon the profile that the client gives you. Some people are happier loaning money. That means you want to loan out your money and you expect to get it back. And you want to be paid interest for loaning it out. Some people are much happier owning a piece of the business and will assume the risk that's there. So I try to sprinkle a little bit of both of them into an account that I manage.

DORSEY: I'd like you to expand on that concept of laddering bonds and explain exactly what that means.

WOODALL: Picture a stepladder that's got five steps to it. Each year you have bonds maturing. For many of my clients, I will set up a ladder of $100,000, $150,000, or $300,000 of maturities each year. We get a printout of monthly cash flow, and I try to space the coupons on the Treasury obligations so that they are getting a check every month. So I have used U.S. Treasuries as a loss leader in laddering, and the customers know that they are safe and secure.

The further you go out, the higher yield will prevail. So if you're looking at short term, usually a year, then the five- or six-year paper will yield more than a one-year piece of paper. The same is true with CDs. When this close-in bond matures, you immediately go out and buy the five-year paper, because whatever that is today, it is the best rate in today's market. We have no idea what interest rates are going to do a year from now, or two, three, four or five. If we average these yields out, we get a yield somewhere in the middle, which is always going to be higher than what it is short term.

There is another method that I use in the fixed income side that I think is an interesting approach. I will barbell fixed income. Let's say we have $500,000. I will take $250,000 of it and ladder it at $50,000 each for five years—one to five years in U.S. Treasuries. Then, I will use the other $250,000 to buy Ginnie Maes, which will always be at a higher rate than what you will get with the five-year paper or on the mortgage securities. So you end up with a barbell effect: a five-year paper at $250,000 that has an average yield, and then $250,000 of long-term yield. And in the middle you average the yields out between the long-term rates and the short-term rate. As the principal comes back in on the Ginnie Maes, it is reinvested at different times into more Ginnie Maes, trying to keep the barbell approach fairly even. This adds constant cash flow to the portfolio.

You can do this with municipal bonds or corporate bonds, but I stick to U.S. Treasuries. So, fixed income is a very good base builder for most brokers. It has a language that a lot of young brokers need to learn. It's something that they can add to their tool kit to distinguish themselves from money managers.

DORSEY: What percentage might you put into a million-dollar account? What would you do with the equities? And how do you go about picking an equity?

WOODALL: Most of the time, I probably have 50 to 60 percent in equity, and 25 to 35 percent fixed incomes, and the rest in cash. And that can vary back and forth depending upon where we are in the market. But the fixed-income side would probably hover around 25 to 35 percent, depending upon the age of the person.

I try to allocate 5 percent in each equity, starting with a 3 percent pilot and building up to 5 to 6 percent. I usually don't want an equity position in the portfolio to exceed 5 to 6 percent in any one particular position. If the fundamentals and the technicals begin to fall into place, I add to the positions and try to increase the weighting up to 5 to 6 percent. Smaller portfolios like $50,000 or $100,000 are going to be higher than 3 to 5 percent. Once they start exceeding 10, 12, 15 percent, I start peeling the weighting down, and start looking for new equity situations.

". . .fixed income is a very good base builder for most brokers. It has a language that a lot of young brokers need to learn."

ROBERT WOODALL

I gear my equity solution on fundamental analysis. I use *Investors Business Daily* as a screening tool. It provides me with statistical information and technical information.

When the earnings rating of a company is 70 percent or higher, you're buying a company that's in the top 30 percent of all the companies reporting earnings.

The next thing that I look at is relative strength. Relative strength numbers can be extremely volatile, so I don't put as much weight in the relative strength numbers as I do in the fundamental numbers. But if I can see the earnings improving, and I know that I've got a stock that's selling at an earnings per share ranking of 55 or 60 or 69, and if I see the relative strength improving on the technical side, then I am probably going to see some improved earnings.

Next, I look at the technical picture from those readings, and I select the stocks that go into portfolios. I constantly update the fundamental news of the stocks that I follow. And I only follow those stocks that are fundamentally recommended by our National Research and my firm, because the market is so big, you can easily dilute yourself with too many different things. I just concentrate on what I know and I use the technical information.

I find that bar charts are much more difficult to interpret than Point and Figure charts. But the thing that's simple about the bar charts are trend lines, so I usually just look at the trend lines and some volume, but I still like to see the basic fundamental formations that I get from Point and Figure.

DORSEY: Let's say you have a Standard & Poor's or *Value Line* sheet. Where do you get your news?

WOODALL: We receive a morning wire from our National Research, which is where most of the fundamental ideas come from. I scan that or take it home that night. If there are companies recommended, then I highlight them, print out information sheets from a print machine, three-hole punch them, and enter them in my research book.

Every day when I see a news article from Dow Jones or *The Wall Street Journal,* then I will print that up from my IOX data machine that sits on my desk. I am always adding to that information. Having that fundamental information there not only keeps me alerted to what's happening, but also allows me to turn around at my desk and open my binder and refresh myself on the situation when a client calls.

DORSEY: You mentioned that you don't allow a position in any one stock to become too large. What do you do in the way of stop limit orders? How do you manage the trade, once you have made the position fundamentally and technically?

WOODALL: I have found that when I put on a position, the first thing I do is project out a 25 to 30 percent profit. I'll just make a note, run portfolios on each one of my accounts, and have them printed out. I'll usually pencil in the first price objective for the stock, and as the stock begins to move up toward that projected 25 to 30 percent, I can put in a reasonable stop place to protect the client with some small profit. Sometimes I will draw a trend line on a bar chart to see the first stop that I can place, as long as it's a profitable trade.

I want my clients to make some money, and I don't want to have a lot of turnover, so I have to be very careful. You can use either the first three box reversal on a Point and Figure chart, or you can look at some trend lines. Let's assume that the position works out. As the stock begins to move up and it hits the first target price, I peel off a third of the position. This is a good tool that I picked up from Dorsey, Wright.

The next price target is 50 percent where I'll peel off a little more. Once the stocks get ahead, I try to give them as much room as possible. I will factor in the bullish support line, and I'll take in the factor of the 200-day moving average. The nature of the business is to build cash and raise the net worth of the portfolio. We are here to build cash, and I don't mean that from the standpoint of cash liquidity, but I am talking about building cash to build net worth in the portfolio.

DORSEY: Do the clients understand this?

WOODALL: I always try to give clients room to create what I call "bragging rights." If you can leave certain stocks in a portfolio that have huge gains, that is something clients can talk about at cocktail parties. I've got very low cost bases in Intel, Microsoft, IBM, Home Depot, and some other stocks. These are things that create trust. It locks clients in because not many brokers let them make big returns in a stock. If they do well, you're going to do well. So the primary concern is always managing the money, managing the risk, and letting your clients make as much money as they possibly can with a minimum amount of risk.

There are good times to be in the market, and there are bad times. I think the Point and Figure with the New York Bullish Percent is always a key barometer of which side you should be on. I have other short-term technical tools that I use that help me in the business, but by and large, knowing where you are at any given point in time in the stock market is critical.

DORSEY: What do you do when you have done all the fundamental work, you have done the technical work, the market is right, the sector is right—and it goes flat against you? How do you manage that type of trade?

WOODALL: There are several components that go into that. Time has a tendency to work a situation out, and if I'm dealing with a long-term bull market, I will keep the stock as an open position.

If the company declines in price to a certain level, I watch for breakouts, a place to do some averaging down. I am not a big believer in this, but it can work to your advantage if you know that the company is going to stay in business. If there is some question of whether the company might not be in business, then you don't want to do this.

I recently bought stock in Electronic Data Systems at higher levels, and they had some bad earnings announcements that dropped it back down to the mid-30s. As soon as it makes a double top and gives the first buy signal coming off of a low, I'll add some more shares. If my initial position was 300 shares, at 42 or 43, I could get stopped out if it falls to 33 or 34. If I get a double top buy at 36, I will buy 100 shares, and for each double top I will add another 100 shares. I will only add to the position if I can improve the cost basis. If it just gives me a double top and I don't improve my cost basis in the overall position, I will not add it. But if they go down, on each double top I will add another 100 shares, not to exceed the usual 5 to 6 percent weighting of the overall portfolio. This is why I mentioned earlier that I usually start with a 3 percent pilot position.

I've also got to have reasonably good fundamentals in stocks I average down in. If not, then I will look for a place where they will rally up so I can take a small loss and get out of them.

I am a firm believer in stop limits rather than stop loss. In the '87 crash, I had some stop losses in, and the markets opened down on that Monday. Big-name stocks were down seven or eight points from where they closed the day before, and if you had stop losses in there, you absolutely got creamed.

Since then, I've used stop limits. Everyone is looking at the same charts. So at a place where a stop should be, they will try to clean out the stops. They will drop them down, trigger and fill your stops at lower levels, and then they will turn around and take them right back up again. When they take them back up, you can get out of the position if you used limits instead of stop losses. And that usually happens within a week after the initial stop has been penetrated.

> *"From a pricing and technical analysis*
>
> *standpoint, there is a tendency to draw*
>
> *the price of a security to a squared number*
>
> *to what is called the 'lure of the square.'"*
>
> ROBERT WOODALL

DORSEY: There is a thing called the "lure of the square" that you have been reluctant to mention to anyone because it's not scientifically proven. I would like you to explain it to me because I think it makes a lot of sense.

WOODALL: That is something that I learned a long time ago. From a pricing and technical analysis standpoint, there is a tendency to draw the price of a security to a squared number to what is called the "lure of the square." Stocks have a tendency to cluster around squared numbers like 81, which can be factored into 9 times 9. Usually when a stock breaks out of a 64 (8 x 8 = 64), 65, 66 level, its next resting place will be 79, 80, 81 (9 x 9 = 81), or 82. So it will tend to cluster around 9 squared, or 81.

They have a tendency to gap a little bit above these numbers. A bad number comes for an earnings report and a stock is 33, 32, 31—in that area. It will go to 25, $24^1/_2$, $23^3/_4$, and then it will come back and sort of lay around the 25 level, which is 5 squared. That's the lure of the square.

Many times, when a stock will break above the 80 level and starts to move to the upper 80s and cross into the 90s, we have made the comment that the stock will usually go to 100. Well, guess what 10 times 10 is? It's 100. That's the lure of the square.

If you look at bar charts or Point and Figure charts, you will see that there is a lot of clustering activity around these particular numbers. I don't know what the magnet is, but it's something just to keep in mind as you buy or sell. These are good places to look for taking profits or putting bids in below the market. I will buy positions many times based upon the technical work and fundamental work, but I will also look at where the lure of the square of that particular stock is. If it is currently at 40 and it's in an uptrend and it's got all the bullish attributes, I'll put some good-till-canceled orders in down at $36^1/_2$, 37. If the market gets hit, I'll be able to pick up those positions at those prices, rather than paying 40 or 41. If I am a seller, I'll put it in to sell at $48^1/_2$ or $49^1/_4$ because it's a square number. Seven times seven is 49. There is nothing scientific about it at all. It's just a phenomenon of the market.

DORSEY: Another tool that you developed years ago was creating a fundamentally normal distribution where you might expect a stock to trade fundamentally from its low to its high. It takes into consideration ratios that go back five years. It's one of the most unique things that I have seen, and I think it could have a lot of relevance for brokers and money managers in this business. Could you explain a little bit about this normal distribution, and where you got the idea?

WOODALL: The idea came out of a book that I read by Kenneth Fisher called *Super Stocks*. Fisher writes about sales ratios. What he did for portfolio work was based upon sales earnings and price-to-sales ratio. If something was selling at seven or eight times its sales, then it was probably at the upper end of a speculative move. Companies' price-to-sales ratios differ because of the types of businesses that they are in. I saw a pattern here when I looked at this particular information along with the *Value Line* statistics (a price-to-sales, price-to-earnings, price-to-book value, price-to-cash flow, and price-to-dividend) to try to come up with some statistical numbers that gave me parameters for what a particular stock can do. So, I divided the sales per year for the past five years and the sales of the company by the high and the low for that period, and I got a medium distribution for each year of the high and the low ratio for sales.

Then I took the *Value Line* estimate of this year, next year's estimate, and applied the average five-year ratio to find the upper end of the high and low ratio for sales. I did that for five years of sales, earnings, dividends, cash flows, and book values and the high and the low ratios. Then I projected it out on a price, and then totaled them to try to get an average of all five of these components.

This formula gave me a way of estimating whether I was paying for an overvalued situation or whether it was priced at fair value or priced at the low end on a five-year historical basis. Keep in mind that there are a lot of variables in here, and that some years a company doesn't earn any money and it shows a loss. If that is not taken into consideration, it will totally distort the figure. But it gives you reasonable parameters of value based upon statistical information that's readily available through *Value Line*.

DORSEY: That's interesting on a fundamental basis because it's not a scientific approach; it's not set in stone. But it makes me feel a little more comfortable when I think of where the Dow might go in the future. It gives me a better feel for the market, and that increases my confidence.

WOODALL: We have to realize that this business is really about individual companies. We all have a tendency to think that this is all paper money. And we sometimes forget that companies are in fact making products or providing services. It's not just a funny money game. The business aspect of what we do is extremely important.

The market psychology is something that we have to deal with all the time. As brokers, we must understand the fundamental business aspect of what these companies do, what they have done in the past, and what their prospects are for the future.

DORSEY: I get the distinct impression by talking to you that the performance game is of no consequence to you. You operate your business by building a relationship with your clients and managing their portfolio to the absolute best of your ability given the information you have available to you.

WOODALL: You're right on target. When I started back in the business again in 1990 as a retail broker, I wanted this to be a ministry. Each day when I drive to work I really pray that there will be people that I can help in some way, whatever that way might be. I have found that if I approach my business that way, I get a great deal more personal satisfaction than I would from outperforming any kind of indices. We investment executives, or whatever you want to call us, are customer men (the root name was "customer man" early in the century). I feel if you build a relationship, the transactions will come.

> *"We have to realize that this business is*
>
> *really about individual companies.*
>
> *We all have a tendency to think that*
>
> *this is all paper money. "*
>
> R O B E R T   W O O D A L L

DORSEY: What do you mean by relationships?

WOODALL: Customers call me for so many different reasons. I am available on any level, at any time, for these people. When I am in their town, I always make sure that I stop by and see them. I don't put clients on hold. When someone calls, they get 100 percent of my time. My conversations are not based upon how much production somebody gives me, but on my relationship with that person as an individual.

We live in a time when there are very few people who will take the time to listen. It's just amazing. I promise that if you build relationships, transactions always come—because people trust you. And, the more they trust you, the more they will give you. If you go in looking to take everything and never give anything, it's going to be difficult.

I can compare business to a pecan tree that we have down here in Texas. When you look at a pecan tree, it's got a tap root that's as long as the tree is tall, and the longer it stays and grows, the deeper the tap root goes. And the deeper the tap root goes, the better it can withstand tremendous storms and the fluctuations of the environment. It's the same way here. If you build your tap root long and strong with good solid business, good tools, good relationships, no matter, good times and bad times, you will have a business that you can be proud of. It can also provide you and your family with an extremely good living.

DORSEY: Those are some very powerful words that I think we can all learn from. If a new broker takes those words to heart, he'll have no trouble building a long-lasting business.

WOODALL: We have the ability not only to be true craftsmen in this industry and provide a product one cannot get anywhere else, but we also have the ability to bring the human element of caring about the people that we deal with every day. That brings a high level of quality to this business that is also personally rewarding.

DORSEY: Thanks, Bob, I learn something every time I talk to you.

A native of Dallas, Texas, and a graduate of Texas Christian University, BOB WOODALL was prepared to enter the ministry. He began his brokerage career with Francis I Du Pont in 1966 as a registered representative in the company's Dallas office. During the 1970s and '80s, he helped to build two New York Stock Exchange member firms and in 1984 became Vice President at Rauscher Pierce. In 1991 he returned to serving his clients full time and remains with Dain Rauscher's Dallas office.

TECHNOLOGY
AND
THE INTERNET

THE CHAPTERS IN THIS BOOK are designed to help brokers position themselves for greater success in this constantly evolving industry; they are intended to give brokers some good ideas to sustain them in the future. One thing is for sure, finance is shaping up to look drastically different in the near future than it does today, and brokers need to be ready.

According to a recent article on *CBS MarketWatch,* by

the end of 1997 investors had opened 3 million accounts at Internet brokerages and that number is expected to grow to 14.4 million by 2002. This figure is astounding if you consider that until just a few years ago brokers controlled all the information. Today, as we know, the Internet is a virtual Disneyland of investment options. What's interesting is that advertisers are increasingly paying for the cost of this information.

Commissions have become a commodity. In fact, according to the MarketWatch article mentioned above, Empire Financial Group actually offers *commission-free* trades on Nasdaq shares of 1,000 or more. Limit orders cost $19.95. Sure Trade offers commission rates of $7.95. The flip side of the coin is that investors are beginning to see what the discounters have missed. There is no registered representative available to assist customers with questions or console them when things get rough.

> *". . .by the end of 1997 investors had opened 3 million accounts at Internet brokerages and that number is expected to grow to 14.4 million by 2002. "*
>
> THOMAS DORSEY

Information is not knowledge. It takes only one misstep on a 1,000-share purchase and the individual investor has used up all the discounts he will get for the rest of his life. Many discount houses have found the price competition fierce. How far below $7.95 can one go and still make money? Price was the lure to investors in the beginning, but now that all discounters are huddled around the basement, they need to come up with other ideas to keep investors interested.

The full-service firms are finding it difficult to compete on price, and the discounters are finding it hard to provide research at their rock-bottom prices. What is likely to develop for full-service firms is a new intermediate level of service, one in which there is a registered representative ready to take orders and discuss investments with investors. The difference is that an investor will get whatever customer service representative is available—similar to when someone calls America OnLine and hears the sweet refrain, "All of our customer representatives are currently assisting other customers. Please wait on line and the first available representative will assist you. The current waiting time is five minutes or less." This will be the discount operation of full-service brokers. Investors will be encouraged to place orders over the Net and download research from the Net as they please. This level of service will be available for a fee which will likely be higher than the average discounter but less than the full service one pays for a personal broker. This is virtually the only way a full service firm will be able to compete for the discount business.

The discounter, on the other hand, will have to rise to a similar level of service by providing research. There is a strange relationship taking place here. Most us think the discounter and the full service outfit are arch rivals with little in common. Well, think again. Some full-service brokerages are selling their coveted research to the discounters so they can provide their clients with research.

This relationship brings the two closer together—they start to look a little more alike. The full-service firm will begin to provide online trading, and the online discounters will offer research. The full service comes down in price, and the discounter comes up in price. Donald Lufkin Jenrette has already entered the online trading arena with the very successful DLJ Direct.

This new segment of broker will be a hybrid of old and new. He will be registered but trained in customer service as well as in traditional securities analysis, stock selection, and portfolio management—a traffic cop, if you will. He will basically manage the flow of information available to the investor as well as handle the questions concerning back office issues and take unsolicited orders. He will not recommend investments or suggest portfolio management options. He will be paid a salary with bonus. This new level will service the customer who periodically wants broker contact but is self-sufficient enough to retrieve his own research from the firm and place the majority of his orders via the Internet. The hard-core do-it-yourselfer will still want the deepest discount with no broker intervention at all.

> *"Information is not knowledge. It takes only one misstep on a 1,000-share purchase and the individual investor has used up all the discounts he will get for the rest of his life."*
>
> THOMAS DORSEY

The good news is that although there are so many different types of brokers to compete with, there are also many more investors today. I don't count full commission brokers out of the game. The best of the best, the most competitive, will continue to do well because there are still a vast number of investors who don't want to, or aren't able to, manage their own portfolios. But some brokers will be cut out of the equation. Traditional, less-progressive brokers who do little more than blindly recommend what their research departments dictate will find business contracting significantly. It is only the full service broker who can consistently make his clients money day in and day out who will continue to flourish in a full commission environment. This broker will need to have more education, motivation, and impeccable integrity in order to flourish. Otherwise, the "Internet Service Desk" awaits.

In order to thrive in the next century, brokers will need to offer more value to their customers. They'll need to learn to use both fundamental and technical analysis, work harder at building relationships and growing business, and carve niches and become more entrepreneurial in how they approach the business. I hope that the examples presented in this book will help brokers move successfully to the next level. We all tell our clients to plan for the future—now it's our turn to devise a plan and follow it into the next generation of finance.

WEB SITES FOR BROKERS

Company Name	Subject	Fee	Web Site
ADR.com	ADRs	none	www.adr.com
Depository Receipt Service	ADRs	none	www.bankofny.com/adr
CANSLIM.net	advisory service	none	www.canslim.net
D. Davis Online Fin. News	advisory service	none	www.dickdavis.com
S&P Personal Wealth	advisory service	fee	www.persoanlwealth.com
First Call Corporation	analyst estimates	fee	www.firstcall.com
Zacks Investment Research	analyst estimates	fee	www.zacks.com
Moody's Investors Service	bond ratings	none	www.moodys.com
Bonds Online	bonds	none	bondsonline.com
Bradynet, Inc.	bonds	none	www.bradynet.com
Investing in bonds.com	bonds	none	www.investinginbonds.com
Rate Net	bonds	none	www.rate.net
US Bur. of Public Debt/Tr	bonds	none	www.publicdebt.treas.gov
Closed End Fund Investor	closed-end funds	fee	www.icefi.com
Hoover's Online	company profiles	none	www.hoovers.com
Annual Report Gallery	company reports	none	www.reportgallery.com
EDGAR Online	company reports	none	www.edgar-online.com
PRARS	company reports	none	www.prars.com

Company Name	Subject	Fee	Web Site
DRIP Central	direct stock purchase	none	www.dripcentral.com
DRIP Investor	direct stock purchase	none	dripinvestor.com
Net Stock Direct	direct stock purchase	none	www.netstockdirect.com
No-Load Stocks Info	direct stock purchase	none	mk.ml.org/noload
InfoBeat—Finance	E-mail service	none	www.infobeat.com
FRB of Atlanta	economic data	none	www.frbatlanta.org
FRB of Boston	economic data	none	www.bos.frb.org
FRB of Chicago	economic data	none	www.frbchi.com
FRB of Cleveland	economic data	none	www.clev.frb.org
FRB of Dallas	economic data	none	www.dallasfed.org
FRB of Kansas City	economic data	none	www.frbkc.org
FRB of Minneapolis	economic data	none	woodrow.mpls.frb.fed.us
FRB of New York	economic data	none	www.ny.frb.org
FRB of Philadelphia	economic data	none	www.phil.frb.org
FRB of Richmond	economic data	none	www.rich.frb.org
FRB of San Francisco	economic data	none	www.frbsf.org
FRB of St. Louis	economic data	none	www.stls.frb.org
Stat-USA	economic data	fee	www.stat-usa.gov
College Savings Bank	educational	none	www.collegesavings.com
William Sharpe's Home Page	educational	none	www-sharpe.stanford.edu
Young Investor	educational	none	www.younginvestor.com
AAII	educational; fund data	fee	www.aaii.com
Adams Owens Kirwan (atty)	estate planning	none	www.estate-planning.net
Estate Plannning Concepts	estate planning	none	www.estateplanning-concepts.com
Estate Planning Learning	estate planning	none	www.estate planning.com
Nolo Press Self Help Law	estate planning	none	www.nolo.com
Trusts, Wills & Estates	estate planning	none	www.wsfpc.com
Wall St. Directory	fin'l service clearinghouse	none	www.wsdinc.com
Briefing.com	finance news	fee	www.briefing.com
CBS MarketWatch	finance news	none	cbs.marketwatch.com
PR Newswire	finance news	none	prnewswire.com

Company Name	Subject	Fee	Web Site
Reuters	finance news	none	www.reuters.com
Barron's	finance news & analysis	fee	www.barrons.com
Bloomberg Financial	finance news & analysis	fee	www.bloomberg.com
Business Week	finance news & analysis	fee	www.businessweek.com
CNN Financial Network	finance news & analysis	none	www.cnnfn.com
Economist	finance news & analysis	fee	www.econmist.com
Financial Times	finance news & analysis	none	www.ft.com
Fortune magazine	finance news & analysis	none	www.pathfinder.com
Kiplinger Online	finance news & analysis	none	www.kiplinger.com
Reality Online Inc.	finance news & analysis	none	www.moneynet.com
WSJ Interactive Edition	finance news & analysis	fee	wsj.com
Investor's Business	finance news &analysis	none	www.investors.com
Fin. Planning Magazine	financial planning	fee	www.fponline.com
Armchair Millionaire	financial planning	none	www.armchairmillionaire.com
Merrill Lynch Inv. Learni	financial planning	none	www.merrill-lynch.ml.com
Prudential	financial planning	none	www.prudential.com
The College for Fin. Plan	financial planning	none	www.fp.edu
Australian Sec. & Inv. Co	foreign investing	none	www.asic.gov.au
Australian Stock Exchange	foreign investing	none	www.asx.com.au
BigCharts Canada	foreign investing	none	canada.bigcharts.com
Emerging Markets Companion	foreign investing	none	www.emgmkts.com
France-Bourse de Paris	foreign investing	none	www.bourse-de-paris.fr
France-Comm de op de bour	foreign investing	none	www.cob.fr
French Governemnt Sec.	foreign investing	none	www.oat.finances.gouv.fr/oat/us
GLOBEfund	foreign investing	none	www.globefund.com
Global Investor	foreign investing	none	www.global-investor.com
Nikkei News English Versi	foreign investing	none	www.nikei.co.jp/enews
PRS Online	foreign investing	fee	www.countrydata.com
Sydney Futures Exchange	foreign investing	none	www.sfe.com.au
Vancouver Stock Exchange	foreign investing	none	www.vse.com
National Fraud Info. Cent	fraud	none	www.fraud.org
Sec. Fraud & Inv. Protect	fraud	none	www.securitieslaw.com
WEBS	index funds &products	none	www.websontheweb.com

Company Name	Subject	Fee	Web Site
Cert, Fin. Planner B. of	invest. professionals	none	www.cfp-board.org
Investor Home	Invest. Web links	none	www.investorhome.com
Nomura Sec.Fin'l Research	investing	none	www.nomura.co.jp/QR
Nelson Invest. Mgmt Netwo	Investmenet professionals	none	www.nelnet.com
Intl, Assoc. for Fin. Pla	Investment professionals	none	www.iafp.org
Money Manager Review	Investment professionals	none	www.slip.net/~mmreview
Natl. Assoc. of Pers. Fin	Investment professionals	none	www.napfa.org
CyberInvest.com	Investment Web links	none	www.cyberinvest.com
InvestorGuide	investment Web links	none	www.investorguide.com
Investorama	investment Web links	none	www.investorama.com
Moneypages	investment Web links	none	www.moneypages.com
Natl. Corporate Services	investment Web links	none	www.natcorp.com/ir
StreetEYE	investment Web links	none	www.efrontier.com
Wall Street Research Net	investment Web links	none	www.wsrn.com
Alert-IPO	IPOs	fee	www.ostman.com/aleret-ipo
Cal Law's IPO Watch	IPOs	none	www.callaw.com/ipo
IPO Central	IPOs	none	www.ipocentral.com
IPO Data Systems	IPOs	fee	www.ipodata.com
IPO Intelligence Online	IPOs	none	www.ipo-fund.com
IPO Maven	IPOs	none	www.ipomaven.com
IPO Monitor	IPOs	fee	www.ipomonitor.com
IPO Prospectus	IPOs	fee	www.ipopro.com
IPO Spotlight Report	IPOs	fee	www.ipospotlight.com
Investor Information Exch	IPOs	none	www.investorx.com
SmallCap Investor	IPOs	none	www.smallcapinvestor.com
BloodHound	life insurance	none	www.bloodhound.com
Conductor B & F Services	life insurance	none	www.conductor.com
InsWeb	life insurance	none	www.insweb.com
Insurance News Network	life insurance	none	www.insure.com
Life Insurance Analysis Clife	insurance	none	www.underwriter.com
Life-Line.org	life insurance	none	www.life-line.com
LifeNet	life insurance	none	www.lifenet.com
QuickQuote	life insurance	none	www.quickquote.com

Company Name	Subject	Fee	Web Site
Quicken Insure Market	life insurance	none	www.insuremarket.com
QuoteShopper	life insurance	none	www.quoteshopper.com
Quotesmith Corp.	life insurance	none	www.quotesmith.com
RightQuote	life insurance	none	www.rightquote.com
Global Financial Data	Market data (historical)	fee	www.globalfindata.com
Moby Data	Market Data (historical)	fee	www.mobydata.com
Pinnacle Data Corp.	market data (historical)	fee	www.pinnacledata.com
Bank Rate Monitor	mortgage calculator	none	www.bankrate.com
Yahoo! Loan Center	mortgage education	none	loan.yahoo.com
AARP Investment Program	mutual funds	none	aarp.scudder.com
ABN AMRO Funds	mutual funds	none	www.abnamrofunds-usa.com
Acorn Funds	mutual funds	none	www.wanger.com
Amcore Funds	mutual funds	none	www.amcore.com
American Century	mutual funds	none	www.americancentury.com
Baron Funds	mutual funds	none	www.baronfunds.com
Berger Funds	mutual funds	none	www.berger funds.com
Bull & Bear Funds	mutual funds	none	www.mutual funds.net
CGM Fund	mutual funds	none	cgmfunds.com
California Investment Tru	mutual funds	none	www.caltrust.com
Calvert Group	mutual funds	none	www.calvertgroup.com
Capstone Funds	mutual funds	none	www.capstonefiancial.com
Columbia Funds	mutual funds	none	www.colombiafunds.com
Crabbe Huson	mutual funds	none	www.contrarian.com
Delafield Fund	mutual funds	none	www.delafield.com
Dreyfus Funds	mutual funds	none	www.dreyfus.com
Dupree Funds	mutual funds	none	www.dupree-funds.com
Eclipse Fund	mutual funds	none	www.townley.com
FAM Funds	mutual funds	none	www.famfunds.com
Fairmont Fund	mutual funds	none	www.fairmontfund.com
Fairport Funds	mutual funds	none	www.fairport.com
Fidelity Investments	mutual funds	none	www.fidelity.com
Flex Funds	mutual funds	none	www.flexfunds.com
Founders Funds	mutual funds	none	www.founders.com

Company Name	Subject	Fee	Web Site
Franklin Templeton	mutual funds	none	www.franklin-templeton.com
Fremont Funds	mutual funds	none	www.fremontfunds.com
Gabelli Funds	mutual funds	none	www.gabelli.com
Galaxy Funds	mutual funds	none	www.galaxyfunds.com
Green Jungle	mutual funds	none	www.greenjungle.com
Homestead Funds	mutual funds	none	www.nreca.org/homestead
IBC Financial Data, Inc.	mutual funds	none	www.ibcdata.com
ICI Mutual Fund Connectio	mutual funds	none	www.ici.org
INVESCO	mutual funds	none	www.invesco.com
Investor Square	mutual funds	none	www.investorsquare.com
Janus	mutual funds	none	www.janus.com
Jones and Babson	mutual funds	none	www.jbfunds.com
Kaufmann	mutual funds	none	www.kaufmann.com
Legg Mason	mutual funds	none	www.leggmason.com
Lindner Funds	mutual funds	none	www.linderfunds.com
Loomis Sayles Funds	mutual funds	none	www.loomissayles.com
Markman Funds	mutual funds	none	www.markman.com
Marshall Funds	mutual funds	none	marshallfunds.com
Maxus Funds	mutual funds	none	maxusfunds.com
Monetta Funds	mutual funds	none	www.monetta.com
Montgomery Funds	mutual funds	none	www.montgomeryfunds.com
Mosaic Funds	mutual funds	none	www.gitfunds.com
Muhlenkamp	mutual funds	none	www.muhlenkamp.com
Mutual Fund Inves. Center	mutual funds	none	www.mfea.com
Mutual Fund Inv. Resource	mutual funds	none	www.fundmaster.com
Mutual Funds Interactive	mutual funds	none	www.fundsintractive.com
Mutual Funds Magazine	mutual funds	fee	www.mfmag.com
Navellier Funds	mutual funds	none	www.navalier.com
Neuberger & Berman	mutual funds	none	www.nbfunds.com
Oak Associates	mutual funds	none	www.oakassociates.com
Oakmark Funds	mutual funds	none	www.oakmark.com
PBHG Funds	mutual funds	none	www.pbhgfunds.com
Papp Funds	mutual funds	none	www.roypapp.com

Company Name	Subject	Fee	Web Site
Pax World Fund	mutual funds	none	www.paxfund.com
Payden & Rygel	mutual funds	none	www.payden.com
Quicken.com	mutual funds	none	www.quicken.com
Robertson Stephens Funds	mutual funds	none	www.rsim.com
Royce Funds	mutual funds	none	www.roycefunds.com
SIT Funds	mutual funds	none	www.sitifunds.com
Safeco Funds	mutual funds	none	www.safecofunds.com
Scout Funds	mutual funds	none	www.umb.com
Scudder Funds	mutual funds	none	www.scudder.com
Selected Funds	mutual funds	none	www.selectfunds.com
Smith Breeden Funds	mutual funds	none	www.smithbreeden.com
Sound Shore Fund	mutual funds	none	www.soundshorefund.com
SteinRoe Funds	mutual funds	none	www.steinroe.com
Strong Funds	mutual funds	none	www.strong-funds.com
T. Rowe Price	mutual funds	none	www.troweprice.com
Third Avenue Value	mutual funds	none	www.mjwhitman.com
United Services Funds	mutual funds	none	www.usfunds.com
Van Wagoner Funds	mutual funds	none	www.vanwagoner.com
Vanguard	mutual funds	none	www.vanguard.com
Vontobel Funds	mutual funds	none	www.vontobelfunds.com
Warburg Pincus Funds	mutual funds	none	www.warburg.com
Wasatch Funds	mutual funds	none	www.wasatchfunds.com
Wayne Hummer Funds	mutual funds	none	www.whummer.com
William Blair Funds	mutual funds	none	www.wmblair.com
Yacktman Funds	mutual funds	none	www.yacktman.com
Delphi Investors Forum	newsgroups	none	www.delphi.com/invest
Raging Bull	newsgroups	none	www.ragingbull.com
A. B. Watley	on-line trading	fee	www. abwatley.com
AccuTrade	on-line trading	fee	www.accutrade.com
AmExp Financial Services	on-line trading	fee	americanexpress.com
Ameritrade	on-line trading	fee	www.ameritrade.com
Andrew Peck Assoc. Inc.	on-line trading	fee	www.andrewpeck.com
Bidwell & Co.	on-line trading	fee	www.bidwell.com

Company Name	Subject	Fee	Web Site
Bull & Bear Securities I	on-line trading	fee	www.bullbear.com
Burke, Christiansen, & Le	on-line trading	fee	www.bclnet.com
Bush Burns Securities	on-line trading	fee	www.bushburns.com
Charles Schwab & Co.	on-line trading	fee	www.schwab.com
CompuTEL Securities	on-line trading	fee	www.computel.com
DLJdirect Financial Netwo	on-line trading	fee	www.dljdirect.com
Datek Online	on-line trading	fee	www.datek.com
Discover Brokerage Direct	on-line trading	fee	www.discoverbrokerage.com
Downstate Discount	on-line trading	fee	www.downstate.com
Dreyfus Brokerage Service	on-line trading	fee	www.edreyfus.com
E'Trade Securities	on-line trading	fee	www.etrade.com
Empire Financial Group	on-line trading	fee	www.lowfees.com
First Flushing Securities	on-line trading	fee	www.firstflushing.com
ForbesNET	on-line trading	fee	www.forbesnet.com
Freedom Investments	on-line trading	fee	www.freedominvestments.com
Freeman Welwood & Co.	on-line trading	fee	www.freemanwelwood.com
InternetTrading.com	on-line trading	fee	www.internettrading.com
Invest Express Online	on-line trading	fee	www.investexpress.com
J.B. Oxford & Co.	on-line trading	fee	www.jboxford.com
Jack White & Co. Online	on-line trading	fee	www.jackwhiteco.com
Max Ule	on-line trading	fee	www.maxule.com
Mr. Stock Online Trading	on-line trading	fee	www.mrstock.com
Muriel Siebert & Co	on-line trading	fee	www.msiebert.com
National Discount Brokers	on-line trading	fee	www.ndb.com
Net Investor	on-line trading	fee	www.netinvestor.com
Newport Discount Brokerag	on-line trading	fee	newport-discount.com
Peremel & Co.	on-line trading	fee	www.peremel.com
ProTrade Securities	on-line trading	fee	www.protrade.com
Quick & Reilly, Inc.	on-line trading	fee	www.quick-reilly.com
Regal Discount Securities	on-line trading	fee	regaldiscount.com
Scottsdale Securities	on-line trading	fee	www.discountbroker.com
Summit Discount Brokerage	on-line trading	fee	www.summitdiscount.com
SureTrade.com	on-line trading	fee	www.suretrade.com

Company Name	Subject	Fee	Web Site
Trade-Well Discount Inves	on-line trading	fee	www.trade-well.com
TradeStar	on-line trading	fee	www.4tradestar.com
Trading Direct	on-line trading	fee	www.tradingdirect.com
WIT Capital	on-line trading	fee	www.witcapital.com
Wall Street Access	on-line trading	fee	www.wsaccess.com
Wall Street Discount	on-line trading	fee	www.wsdc.com
Waterhouse Securities	on-line trading	fee	www.waterhouse.com
Web Street Securities	on-line trading	fee	www.webstreetsecurities.com
Your Discount Broker	on-line trading	fee	www.ydb.com
Ziegler Thrift Trading	on-line trading	fee	www.investroute.com
(CBOE)	options/futures	none	www.cboe.com
Chicago Board of Trade	options/futures	none	www.cbot.com
Chicago Mercantile Exchange	options/futures	none	www.cme.com
Coffee, Sugar & Cocoa Ex	options/futures	none	www.csce.com
Commodity Fut. Tr. Comm.	options/futures	none	www.cftc.gov
Commodity Systems Inc.	options/futures	fee	www.csidata.com
Futures Trading Group	options/futures	none	www.futurestrading.com
Investment Research Inst.	options/futures	none	www.options-iri.com
MidAmerica Commodity Exch	options/futures	none	www.midam.com
National Futures Association	options/futures	fee	www.nfa.futures.org
New York Cotton Exchange	options/futures	none	www.nyce.com
New York Mercantile Exch.	options/futures	none	www.nymex.com
PowerOptions	options/futures	fee	www.poweropt.com
Consomer Information Cent	persoanl finance	none	www.pueblo.gsa.gov/
Financenter.com	personal finance	none	www.financecenter.com
Investment FAQ	personal finance	none	www.invest-faq.com
Money.com	personal finance	none	jcgi.pathfinder.com/money/ plus/index.oft
Quicken Financial Network	personal finance	none	www.qfn.com
InfoFund	portfolio tracking	none	www.infofund.com
Investools	portfolio tracking	fee	www.investools.com
League of American Invest	portfolio tracking	none	www.investorsleague.com
nVestor	portfolio tracking	none	investorsleague.com

Company Name	Subject	Fee	Web Site
Stock Smart	portfolio tracking	none	www.stocksmart.com
Resicom Analytics	real estate	fee	www.resicom.com
Amer. Institute of CPAs	regulations	none	www.aicpa.org
Fed. Deposit Insur. Corp	regulations	none	www.fdic.gov
Federal Trade Commision	regulations	none	www.ftc.gov
NASD Regulation Inc.	regulations	none	www.nasdr.com
(NASD)	regulations	none	www.nasd.com
NASAA	regulations	none	www.nasaa.org
SEC Law.com	regulations	none	www.seclaw.com
(SEC)	regulations	none	www.sec.gov
NAREIT Online	REITs	none	www.nareit.com
RealtyStocks	REITs	none	www.realitystocks.com
Securities Industry Assoc	securities industry	none	www.sia.com
OTC Financial Network	small stock profiles	none	www.otcfn.com
Stockguide	smallstock profiles	none	www.stockguide.com
Co-op America	social concerns	none	www.coopamerica.org
Good Money	social concerns	none	www.goodmoney.com
GreenMoney On-Line Guide	social concerns	none	www.greenmoney.com
Social Investment Forum	social concerns	none	www.socialinvest.org
Social Security Online	Social Security	none	www.ssa.gov
Dial/Data	stock & fund quotes	fee	www.tdc.com/ddhp.html
BigCharts	stock charts & analysis	none	www.bigcharts.cocm
MarketEdge	stock charts & analysis	fee	www.stkwtch.com
.xls	stock data	fee	www.xls.com
Dow Jones Markets	stock data	none	www.djmarkets.com
Hoover's Stockscreener	stock data	none	www.stockscreener.com
MarketGuide	stock data	none	www.marketguide.com
Media General Fin. Services	stock data	none	www.mgfs.com
myTrack	stock data	none	www.mytrack.com
WallSt.com	stock data	fee	www.walst.com
Dorsey, Wright & Associates	stock data & analysis	fee	www.dorseywright.com
Equity Analytics	stock data & analysis	none	www.e-analytics.com
Motley Fool	stock data & analysis	none	www.fool.com

Company Name	Subject	Fee	Web Site
Primark Invest. Research	stock data & analysis	fee	www.pirc.com
Quote.Com	stock data & analysis	fee	www.quote.com
American Stock Exchange	stock exchange	none	www.amex.com
Chicago Stock Exchange	stock exchange	none	chicagostockex.com
Kansas City Board of Trade	stock exchange	none	www.kcbt.com
Nasdaq Stock Market	stock exchange	none	www.nasdaq.com
New York Stock Exchange	stock exchange	none	www.nyse.com
Philadelphia Stock Exchange	stock exchange	none	www.phlx.com
Bull Session	stock quotes	fee	www.bullsession.com
InterQuote	stock quotes	fee	www.interquote.com
MoneyScope	stock quotes	none	www.moneyscope.com
Thomson Real Time Quotes	stock quotes	none	www.thomson.rtq.com
WWQuote	stock quotes	fee	www.wwquote.com
Wall Street City	stock screening	none	www.wallstreetcity.com
TheStreet.com	stock/fund & quotes	fee	www.thestreet.com
Data Broadcasting Corp.	stock/fund data	none	www.dbc.com
Microsoft Investor	stock/fund data	fee	www.investor.msn.com
Morningstar Net	stock/fund data	fee	www.morningstar.net
Prophet Information Services	stock/fund data	fee	www.prophetdata.com
Stock Data Corp.	stock/fund data	fee	www.stockdata.com
StockMaster	stock/fund data	none	www.stockmaster.com
Thomson Investors Network	stock/fund data	fee	www.thomsoninvest.net
V-Line Inv. Res & Asset M	stock/fund data	none	www.valueline.com
Worden Brothers Online	stock/fund data	fee	www.tc2000.com
Stockpoint	stock/fund data & analysis	none	www.stockpoint.com
Yahoo! Finance	stock/fund data & analysis	none	quote.yahoo.com
Daily Stocks	stock/fund quotes	none	www.dailystocks.com
1040.Com	tax information	none	www.1040.com
Deloitte & Touche	tax information	none	www.dtonline.com
E & Y T & F Planning	tax information	none	www.wiley.com/ey
H&R Block	tax information	none	www.hrblock.com

Company Name	Subject	Fee	Web Site
IRS	tax information	none	www.irs.ustreas.gov
Microsoft Money Insider	tax information	none	moneyinsider.msn.com
Net Tax 9X	tax information	none	www.nettax.com
SecureTax	tax information	none	www.securetax.com
Tax Foundation	tax information	fee	www.taxfoundation.org
Tax Help Online	tax information	none	www.taxhelponline.com
Tax Library	tax information	fee	www.taxlibrary.com
Tax Logic	tax information	none	www.taxlogic.com
Tax Prophet	tax information	none	www.taxprophet.com
Tax Tips and Facts	tax information	none	www.rak-l.com
Taxing Times	tax information	fee	www.maxwell.com/tax
Taxwizard	tax information	none	taxwizard.com
TurboTax Online	tax information	none	www.turbotax.com
ASK Research Stock	technical analysis	none	www.askresearch.com
EQUIS International	technical analysis	none	www.equis.com
IQC.com	technical analysis	none	www.iqc.com
Market Technicians Assoc.	technical analysis	none	www.mta-usa.org
News.com Investor	technical analysis	none	www.news.com/investor
Technical Analysis Charti	technical analysis	none	www.alphachart.com
Timely.com	technical analysis	none	www.timely.com
Silicon Investor	technology stocks	none	www.techstocks.com

USED WITH PERMISSION from the American Association of Individual Investors, 625 N. Michigan Ave., Chicago, IL 60611 (800-428-2244; 312-280-0170)

THE BASICS OF POINT & FIGURE CHARTING

THE CORNERSTONE OF DORSEY, WRIGHT research is technical analysis, more specifically Point & Figure charting. Fundamental research tells what ought to happen, while technical research tells us what is happening and indicates the future probabilities.

In other words, the Point & Figure chart answers the question of *when* to buy and *when* to sell.

Top-Down Approach to Investing

WE USE OUR PRIMARY market indicators to get a measure of overall risk. Dorsey, Wright uses technical market indicators which have been in existence for almost forty years to ascertain the overall risk in the market—to determine whether offense or defense is dictated. We then analyze our broad industry sectors to determine which sector or sectors have good field position. Industry sectors move in and out of season just like produce in the supermarket. We then select individual stocks that have positive relative strength and have a good probability of outperforming the market. In other words, demand is in control.

There is always a time to buy and a time to sell even the most attractive security. In fact, it is our belief that avoiding severe losses is more important in determining overall market performance over the course of an entire market cycle.

We follow over 8,000 stocks daily, permitting us great agility and timing in making investment recommendations.

Point and Figure Chart Basics

POINT AND FIGURE CHARTS are indigenous to stock market trading, giving both the immediate and long-term view. Point and Figure charts date back to the late 1800s and Charles Dow. The Point and Figure chart is a logical, sensible, and organized way of recording the supply and demand relationship in any stock. The Point and Figure chart ignores the static time factor, the confusing volume indications, and irrelevant minor fluctuations.

The basic Point and Figure chart shows a column of Xs, which means the stock or index is rising. A column of Os means the stock is falling. Columns of Xs and Os alternate back and forth—they never appear in the same column. For the first action taken in a month, a number or letter is used to designate that particular month. This is how we show the time on the chart.

It takes three boxes to reverse from one direction to the other. For example, if a stock were trading in a column of Xs with a top of 45, it would take a move to 42 to reverse this chart to a column of Os. Going in the other direction, if a stock were trading in a column of Os with a current low at 45, it would need a rally to 48 to reverse the stock back to a column of Xs.

Units of Charting

0 - 5	= 1/4 point per box
$5^1/_2$ - 20	= 1/2 point per box
21 - 100	= 1 point per box
102 and up	= 2 points per box

Daily Charting

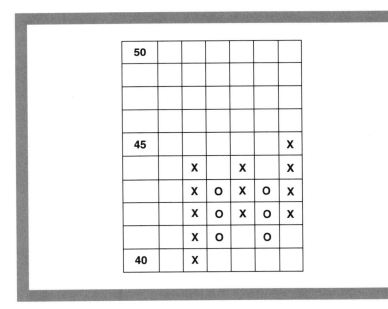

ABOVE WE HAVE A Point and Figure chart of XYZ. Every day we will look at the high and low price to determine if a change needs to be made on the chart. Let's go through an example of how we would chart XYZ.

Since the last entry on the chart is an X, we first check the stock's daily high. Add Xs if the stock has gone up one or more units on your grid. If the stock has gone down, look at the daily low to see if a three-box reversal has occurred. If so, move over one column and down one row and enter the appropriate number of Os. Make no chart entry if the stock has not moved up enough to warrant more Xs or down enough to receive at least three Os. (In the example above, first check to see if the chart can move up another box to 46. If not, see if it can reverse down three boxes to 42 (45 - 3).

If the last entry on the chart is an O, check the stock's daily low. Add Os if the stock has gone down one or more units on your grid. If the stock has gone up, look at the daily high to see if a three-box reversal has occurred. If so, move over one column and up one row and enter the appropriate number of Xs. Make no chart entry if the stock has not moved down enough to warrant more Os or up enough to receive at least three Xs.

Chart Patterns

CHART PATTERNS ARE the backbone of Point and Figure charting. The formations accurately record the battle between supply and demand. There are two basics chart patterns, the double top and the double bottom. Every other pattern is just a variation on the double top and double bottom. Pages 240 through 243 show chart examples of some of the more frequent Point and Figure patterns, and a brief description of each.

TRENDLINES

USING TRENDLINES HELPS us to make buy/sell decisions. When a trendline is broken, it signals a change in the posture of the stock. The two major trendlines—the bullish support line and the bearish resistance line—can be used to identify areas of support and resistance in Point and Figure charts. As long as a stock is trading above the bullish support line, we say the main trend is positive. If the stock is trading below the bearish resistance line, the main trend of the stock is negative.

◆ **Bullish Support Line:** When the stock has formed an apparent bottom, a bullish support line can be drawn. It should start in the box directly below the lowest O in the lowest column and move upward at a 45-degree angle.

◆ **Bearish Resistance Line:** This is the reciprocal of the bullish support line. A bearish resistance line is to be drawn above the highest X in the highest column downward at a 45-degree angle.

Relative Strength

RELATIVE STRENGTH READINGS are incredibly important in stock selection in all kinds of markets. The relative strength calculation is simply done by dividing the price of the stock by the price of the Dow or any index you choose and then multiplying by 1,000. This number can then be plotted on a Point and Figure chart. RS chart buy signals are given when a column of Xs exceeds a previous column of Xs. Sell signals are given when a column of Os exceeds a previous column of Os. Relative strength signals generally last about two years and tell the overall trend of a stock. Positive relative strength suggests the stock will outperform the market while negative relative strength suggests the stock will underperform the market. It's also important to watch for reversals and which column the stock is currently in for short-term guidance.

Say, for instance, XYZ was at $80 and the Dow was at 9,000. If we divided $80 by 9,000 and moved the decimal we would get 8.89. This number can be plotted just as if it was an $8 stock. Let's say the following week the stock falls to $75 and the Dow dropped to 8,000. We now divide $75 by 8,000 and get 9.38. In this case the stock dropped, the Dow dropped, but the relative strength chart went up. This tells us that the stock is doing better than the Dow and the only reason it is down is that the overall market is down. This stock will be one of the first to snap back when the overall market is ready. Remember 75 to 80 percent of the risk in a stock is market risk, 20 to 25 percent is stock specific risk.

NYSE Bullish Percent

THIS IS OUR MAJOR market indicator telling us whether to be on the offense or defense. It is calculated by dividing the number of NYSE stocks trading on Point and Figure buy signals by the total listed on the Exchange. The percent of stocks on buy signals in is then plotted on a grid from 0 percent to 100 percent, where each box equals 2 percent. Levels above 70 percent are generally considered overbought, and below 30 percent are considered oversold. The best buy signals come when the NYSE Bullish Percent goes below 30

Bullish Chart Patterns

Double Top

			X		
			X		
35			B		
	X		X		
	X	O	X		
	X	O	X		
	X	O			
30					

An X (up) column exceeds the previous X (up) column. The simplest of all buy signals.

Triple Top

45							
						X	
						X	
						B	
						X	
40						X	
			X		X	X	
			X	O	X	O	X
			X	O	X	O	X
				O		O	
35							

An X column exceeds two previous columns, or levels of resistance.

Bullish Catapult

45										
							X			
							3			
							X			
						X	X			
35						X	O	X		
			X		X	X	O	X		
			X	O	X	O	X	O		
			X	O	X	O	X			
				O		O				
30										

Combination of a triple top buy signal followed by a double top buy signal.

Shakeout

50									
					X				
					X				
					X				
		X		X	X				
45		X	O	X	O	X			
		X	O	X	O	X			
		X	O	X	O	X			
		X	O		O	X			
		X			O				
40									

Stock makes two tops, then breaks a double bottom. This rids stock of weak holders. Can buy on three box reversal up. Shakeout is completed when triple top is broken.

Bullish Triangle

40					X				
					X				
		X			B				
		X	O		X				
		X	O	X	X				
35		X	O	X	O	X			
		X	O	X	O	X			
		X	O	X	O				
		X	O	X					
		X	O						
30		X							

Series of lower tops and higher bottoms. Chart breaks out one way or the other. Take action on breakout, but not until then. Five columns are required to make the pattern.

Bearish Chart Patterns

Double Bottom

45						
			X			
		O	X	O		
		O	X	O		
		O		O		
40				O		
				O		
				O		

An O (down) column exceeds the previous O (down) column.
The simplest of all sell signals.

Triple Bottom

45							
			X		X		
		O	X	O	X	O	
		O	X	O	X	O	
		O		O		O	
40						O	
						4	
						O	

An O column exceeds two previous columns, or levels of
support.

Bearish Catapult

45									
			X		X				
		O	X	O	X	O			
		O	X	O	X	O	X		
		O		O		O	X	O	
40						O	X	O	
						O		O	
								O	
								8	
								O	
35								O	

Combination of triple bottom sell signal followed by double bottom sell signal.

Bearish Triangle

50									
		O							
		O	X						
		O	X	O					
		O	X	O	X				
45		O	X	O	X	O			
		O	X	O	X	O			
		O	X	O		O			
		O				O			
						O			
40						O			

Similar to the bullish triangle, but double bottom is broken to manifest bearish signal. Once again, wait for the double bottom to initiate positions.

percent and then reverses up (must reverse 6 percent). The best sell signals come when the indicator moves above 70 percent and then reverses below 70 percent. Not only does the NYSE Bullish Percent tell us which team to have on the field, it also tells us what our field position is. There are also six degrees of risk associated with this indicator:

1 Bull Alert. Characterized by the bullish percent falling to 30 percent or below and then reversing up into a column of Xs. The traffic light turns green.

2 Bull Confirmed. The strongest of market conditions. Characterized by a column of Xs exceeding a previous column of Xs. The traffic light is green.

3 Bull Correction. The bull market is taking a breather, though it should resume shortly. The traffic light is yellow.

4 Bear Alert. Characterized by a bullish percent falling from above 70 percent to below. Profits should be taken or positions hedged. The traffic light has turned red.

5 Bear Confirmed. The weakest of market conditions. Characterized by a column of Os exceeding a previous column of Os. The traffic light is red.

6 Bear Correction. The bear market is taking a breather. Trading rallies could be seen but the bear market will likely resume. The traffic light is flashing red—look both ways carefully before crossing the intersection.

Remember, when evaluating any particular risk level, be sure to take into consideration the field position.

Sector Bullish Percents

USING THE SAME CONCEPT as the NYSE Bullish Percent, we keep bullish percent charts of each of the forty-two industry groups. The percent of stocks on buy signals in each sector is plotted on a grid from 0 percent to 100 percent. As with the NYSE bullish percent, the best buy signals come when a sector goes below 30 percent and then reverses up. The best sell signals come when a sector goes above 70 percent and then reverses below 70 percent. The same six risk levels apply.

Short Term Indicators

◆ **NYSE Percent of Stocks above Their Ten-Week Moving Average:** Charted on the same type of grid as the bullish percents. Buy signals are given when the index goes below 30 percent and reverses up, as well as when a column of Xs exceeds a previous column of Xs. Sell signals are given when the index goes above 70 percent and reverses down, as well as when a column of Os exceeds a previous column of Os.

◆ **NYSE High-Low Index:** This index measures the number of new highs made on the NYSE divided by the number of new highs plus new lows. This number is then recorded on a ten-day moving average. The ten-day moving average is then plotted on a grid from 0 percent to 100 percent. We look at the percent of stocks above their ten-week moving average and the NYSE High-Low Index in conjunction with one another. Buy signals are given when the index goes below 30 percent and reverses up, as well as when a column of Xs exceeds a previous column of Xs. Sell signals are given when the index goes above 70 percent and reverses down, as well as when a column of Os exceeds a previous column of Os.

Bond Indicator

◆ **Dow Jones 20 Bond Average:** A long-term bond indicator, which helps weigh the advantages of holding interest-rate-bearing securities. This average is plotted on a Point and Figure chart with a box size of .20. The average moves slow and does not often give signals, but when they occur, we pay attention. A sell signal, which is given when a column of Os exceeds a previous column of Os, suggests that rates are about to rise. The opposite holds for buy signals.

INDEX

About Bloomberg

Bloomberg L.P., founded in 1981, is a global information services, news, and media company. Headquartered in New York, the company has nine sales offices, two data centers, and 80 news bureaus worldwide.

Bloomberg Financial Markets, serving customers in 100 countries around the world, holds a unique position within the financial services industry by providing an unparalleled combination of news, information, and analytic tools in a single package known as the BLOOMBERG® service. Corporations, banks, money management firms, financial exchanges, insurance companies, and many other entities and organizations rely on Bloomberg as their primary source of information.

BLOOMBERG NEWS^{SM}, founded in 1990, offers worldwide coverage of economies, companies, industries, governments, financial markets, politics, and sports. The news service is the main content provider for Bloomberg's broadcast media, which include BLOOMBERG TELEVISION®—the 24-hour cable television network available in ten languages worldwide—and BLOOMBERG NEWS RADIO™—an international radio network anchored by flagship station BLOOMBERG NEWS RADIO AM 1130^{SM} in New York.

In addition to the BLOOMBERG PRESS® line of books, Bloomberg publishes *BLOOMBERG® MAGAZINE, BLOOMBERG PERSONAL FINANCE™*, and *BLOOMBERG WEALTH MANAGER™*.

To learn more about Bloomberg, call a sales representative at:

Frankfurt:	49-69-920-410
Hong Kong:	852-977-6000
London:	44-171-330-7500
New York:	1-212-318-2000
Princeton:	1-609-279-3000
San Francisco:	1-415-912-2960
São Paulo:	5511-3048-4500
Singapore:	65-438-8585
Sydney:	61-29-777-8686
Tokyo:	81-3-3201-8900

About Dorsey, Wright & Associates

DORSEY, WRIGHT & ASSOCIATES is an independent and privately owned registered investment advisory firm whose business includes two areas: investment research services for numerous broker-dealers and large institutions around the world, and professional management of equity portfolios for investors.

The two principals of the firm, Thomas J. Dorsey and Watson H. Wright, have extensive experience in the equity markets, particularly in the field of risk management, for which they are known internationally. Combined, Mr. Dorsey and Mr. Wright have over 40 years of experience in the equity and options markets. This record of longevity enables them to consistently and correctly analyze and interpret the investment climate.

Dorsey, Wright research is conducted along technical lines, adhering to the relationship between supply and demand. We believe this simple but accurate economic theory is manifested as a constant battle between these two forces for control of the equity vehicle. It is this objective, logical approach which helps reduce uncertainty in the market.

One of the most important ingredients of success in this business is confidence. Dorsey, Wright & Associates' research will give you strength in your convictions and provide you with an orderly, systematic approach to investing.

For more information on Tom Dorsey and Dorsey, Wright & Associates, click on the Web site at **www.dorseywright.com.**